All
Madly
Educational

by

Brian French

Grosvenor House
Publishing Limited

The right of Brian French to be identified as the author of this
work has been asserted in accordance with Section 78
of the Copyright, Designs and Patents Act 1988

The book cover picture is copyright to Brian French

This book is published by
Grosvenor House Publishing Ltd
28-30 High Street, Guildford, Surrey, GU1 3EL.
www.grosvenorhousepublishing.co.uk

A CIP record for this book
is available from the British Library

ISBN 978-1-78148-398-5

Contents

Acknowledgements

I would like to thank:

St Helens Connect and in particular 'Robbob' and permission to use his photographs. All other photographs are the author's or from Wikipedia.

Graham French, my cousin, for his St Helens input and advice.

Plus Richard French, Craig Sefton and Ruth White who gave the book the once over.

I apologise to all those team members whose names I have forgotten.

Author's Prologue

In January 1940, as Adolf Hitler was planning the destruction of the free world, I chose to be born. Fortunately I knew very little about it and more fortunately I was born in the outskirts of St Helens, which although being only 12 miles from Liverpool and its shattered docks and gutted buildings, saw very little enemy action. After the initial scurrying to the shelter at the sound of the air raid warning, most residents of the Carr Mill district stayed in their homes. The only 'damage' we witnessed was after the war, when the 'wrecking ball', used to demolish the concrete shelters, also destroyed Old Man Bryant's front wall. My dad was called up in 1942 and was drafted to take part in the D-Day landings, but fortunate again, was 'stood down' at the last minute, after two weeks 'embarkation leave', and fought the Germans from rural Bicester until he was demobbed. All over England little children were embarrassing their young mothers by asking, 'Is that my dad?' when any khaki clad figure walked by.

Sometimes it was.

As many emergency measures were put in place during the war, married women were allowed to continue working. My mum was a teacher or to put it in context, 'This teacher was my mum'. So I began my education at the age of three and a half in the Nursery Department of Parr Flat School, where she taught Juniors. This entailed getting up in the pitch-black morning (Double Summer Time) and taking two buses to the other side of town. There was also the gross indignity of having to 'have a nap' in the nursery every afternoon. When dad was demobbed, mum had just got into her stride and, now as the main earner, carried on teaching nearer to home. She was the teacher par excellence, born for the job. She taught me, she taught my mates, she taught at Sunday School. Her cry, 'Whatever am I going to do for Handwork tomorrow?' would ring through the house. She was also a pianist and had the disconcerting ability to stand up while playing and peer over the top of the piano to spot fidgeting children.

Dad was a complete contrast, an amiable, working class Lancastrian who strolled effortlessly through life, and could take the sting out of Mum's earnestness i.e., come to my rescue. He was my idol. He was funny, could do tricks, and was very fit and agile. He could do one handed press-ups and jump over his own foot. He had a charismatic appeal for children; my mates used to call round to see 'if Mr French could play out'. Yet he was very 'proper' and I never heard him swear. 'Sweet Night' was his only expletive. He could always make my mum laugh even after the most torrid exchanges. 'Never let the sun go down upon thy wrath', was one of his many saws. 'Consider the lilies of the field' was another, especially when mum wanted him to 'get off his backside'.

Gwen and Alf, mater and pater, in Sunday best, headgear compulsary.

With this background I roared happily through my early days, excelling at school and in sport. I loved every minute of it and at the end of my junior school life, I can distinctly remember feeling a sort of confidence that I had 'arrived' as a person. And now read on...

A leap into the future? The author clears 3ft 11in at St Helens Junior School Sports.

Preface

I have taken my title from the opening chapter of David Kynaston's epic work on the 1950's, *Family Life*. It is a throwaway comment from the late Kenneth Williams on his thoughts about the exhibits and themes of the Festival of Britain, staged on London's South Bank in 1951. This phrase could not be more appropriate to describe the lives of countless school children, who in that same year embarked on a journey, which would shape their future lives – entry into the Grammar School system. The experience was 'educational' and at times completely 'mad', facing a collection of mentors who ranged from 'slightly eccentric' to 'totally barking'. And yet, just as the 1951 Festival of Britain with its iconic Skylon and The Dome of Discovery was, for our parents, something new and vibrant for them after the long years of war, and the longer years of rationing, so coincidently for us, entrance to the Grammar School was our golden opportunity, if we took it, to make our mark and go beyond anything our parents had been able to achieve.

Many 'naysayers' such as the historian Corelli Barnett, never cease to tell us that the country was completely bankrupt after the war, with the Empire in decline, and America calling for the repayment of its War Loans, and that whatever the Government introduced was window dressing or worse – financial irresponsibility in the case of the 'free' National Health System. So the idea of a Festival was ridiculous and obviously 'doomed to failure'. The current joke was that the Skylon, the striking symbol of the Festival, with no visible means of support, was 'just like the economy'. But looking back, I found it far more uplifting to think of myself as a 'New Elizabethan' with a life of discovery in front of me. I don't think that any child who had tasted his first banana or her first pineapple, at the age of seven, could think any differently. Things were going to be better, and by and large they were. Of course, as 'innocents', we were unaware that 'the peace' was just as problematic for our leaders as 'the war'. We were just thankful for the chance to have a childhood.

Beginnings

On a bright morning in early September 1951, I, along with 89 other confident, or shy, or boisterous, or terrified eleven-year-old boys, took my place on the long balcony overlooking the main hall of Cowley Boys' Grammar School, St Helens. The smell of new leather satchels and clothing, hung in the air. Down below us in the body of the Hall sat 'The School'; 500 boys in all. Out at the front, stood a commanding, gowned, almost godlike figure with wavy blond hair. This was not a master but the Head Boy, 'Neddie' Naylor, (he actually *spoke* to me once). From time to time this figure issued odd injunctions, 'Settle down, *Parthians,*' or 'This is your last warning, *Etruscans*'. We soon learned that he was addressing two of the eight 'Houses' into which the school was divided for assembly and all intra

The school in a sylvian setting.

school competitions. The 'tribes' were *Celts, Etruscans, Parthians, Romans, Spartans, Teutons, Trojans, and Vikings*. (I became a very proud *Viking* – colours gold and black – mascot a raven.)

Somewhere below us in the distance a door slammed. More strange activity; everyone stood up in silence. We were waved to our feet by smiling staff. Urgent footsteps on polished wood; and onto the raised stage strode a smart grey headed man in a black gown, the Headmaster, Albert Cantle MA, lord of the known universe and controller of our fates. Our new life was about to begin. Mr Cantle had a unique stage delivery (well it was pre Gordon Brown) which consisted of pausing in mid

The crest of Viking House

sentence, looking upward with open mouth, rotating his head to the right and then continuing his peroration. This 'pause for effect' tactic brought him an unwelcome response from the school some time later. One morning, when we were doing Jethro Tull's seed drill or some such in History, three bells were rung in the quadrangle. This signified an extraordinary assembly in the hall and a chance to down tools. Usual buzz of speculation; 'Settle down *Romans*' etc; door bangs; in comes Cantle; so far so normal. Then Albert got into his stride. He asked that all the women staff and female secretarial staff should leave the assembly. Absolute silence; what one earth had happened? (I suppose that within the deep recesses of our ever guilty childish minds we all thought, 'Is it me?') He then began, 'I have called (pause, look up) this assembly (pause, look up) because someone (pause, lookup) has written (pause, look up, pause, pause) **SHIT** on...' He obviously misjudged his audience as the explosion of laughter from 500 oiks destroyed his solemnity. I cannot for the life of me recall what happened next – but who cares. I was there.

Cowley School was, of its time, a magnificent, state of the art, school building. Fortunate to have been completed just before WWII, it was a proud four-square edifice of Lancashire red brick. Although it had suffered the (unnecessary) depredation of its iron railings in order to build bombers for Britain, its frontage looked confidently across well-tended lawns to Hard Lane, which also boasted the grounds of the St Helens and District Cemetery opposite. Any symbolism about golden lads all coming to dust was lost on us but we did know that our school was at the dead centre of town (weak first year joke). Arranged round a lawned internal quadrangle, only to be crossed by staff and prefects, were three floors of classrooms, laboratories, workshops, a gymnasium, art room, music room, library, showers, an *indoor* bike shed – the works. Outside was the huge cricket field/athletics track, then up a bank to the school canteen and on to the wild expanse of The Top Field, then an undeveloped piece of land. Further up Hard Lane, a short journey in our clicking studded football boots, was an even larger expanse of green, housing several Rugby pitches and the 'home' of the First XV.

To be part of this community and wear 'the maroon and grey' gave you a sense of pride. This was what 'passing the scholarship' i.e. the eleven-plus examination meant, and made all those 'mental arithmetic' tests and '10 Spellings' on alternate mornings at your Junior School worth while. Thankfully, we were not aware of the controversy that the 1944 Butler Act and 'the tripartite system' had stirred up, or that the eventual abolition of this so called 'divisive exam' would be the 'saviour of the country's education system', as all Left leaning politicians and academics so firmly believed – as they set about wrecking it. For them, the new Comprehensives would sweep away the class ridden system and equal opportunity for all would be the key. Would it were so. Today, with families moving house and/or paying to get their children into any school which can raise itself beyond the 'bog standard comp', the system seems to have been put firmly into reverse. *Si monumentum requiris cicumspice.*

For us, the 'eleven-plus' was an exam that we 'sat' with the promise (but not in my case) of a bike if you 'passed'. No one seemed too bothered about not going to Cowley. If you were 'clever' you would go. If you were 'normal' you wouldn't. There was bit of ribbing, 'Cowley Custards' was a favourite, but we all still played football together and carried on as usual. The idea that somehow the system *penalized* working class children was just untenable. St Helens was a working class town with mining and glass comprising its two major industries, supported by evil smelling ammonia and gas works. The Sankey Navigation, the first industrial canal opened in Britain, wended its gloomy way through the town. Rugby League, the North's answer to the Union code, dominated the sporting scene. We were working class children and we were offered our chance. Kynaston confirms 'few parents were hostile to the whole system, many were indifferent, and a growing minority very enthusiastic'. There were of course exceptions. The mother of one of our 'gang' was so furious that her beloved son had not 'passed' that she hauled him off to a 'crammers' in Liverpool and all contact with us was severed.

A poem that featured in *The Cowleian* of June 1960, the annual school magazine, will give both the flavour of St Helens (and Lancashire whimsy). It was penned by a pupil A.I. Winstanley, who went on to read English at Leeds.

Twixt Liverpool and Manchester
Set midst emerald hills
St Helens nestles, sombre, grim
The home of Beecham's Pills

Its interesting feature
Is its lack of cultural wealth
Nor is it recommended for
Improvement of the health

You'll not hear Shakespeare mentioned
Art Galleries we have none

The tele' reigns supreme, and so
The Theatre too is gone**

A hundred factory chimneys
Eternal guardians are
Of places with romantic names
Like Greenbank, Sutton, Parr

Yet, go to hallowed Knowsley Road
Some winter Saturday
And see the thousands flock to watch
Their burly heroes play

Oh, sorrow not St Helens
For oft I think of thee
Of the lovely golden sunsets
O'er the tin roofed UGB*

When I think of stark, high slagheaps
My heart with pleasure fills
And my soul doth start a dancing
In the home of Beecham's Pills

---

*U.G.B was the home of United Glass Bottles one of the many glass manufacturers of
the town.
** It's back now!

The iconic clock tower of Beecham's Pills

A typical industrial landscape by Robbob

(For anyone wishing to read of St Helens in her full majesty, I recommend Alan Tucker's (2014) book about growing up in post war St Helens. While we trod the same paths, – this author appears on Alan's Cowley School's Sports Day Programme (Senior Hurdles. Lane 2) – his canvas is broader than mine.)

Early Days in 3B

As first year pupils we were put into Form 3. This was strange but it was explained that in former times Cowley used to have a preparatory school unit for younger boys i.e. Years 1 and 2. So that was fine. After Form 3 you went into Form 4 then? Oh no, you went into 'Shell' (despite my natural curiosity I never asked why) and then on to the third year, which was called, wait for it, Form 4. In year 4 you went into 'the Remove' (don't ask). It was an anti-climax to get into year Five, and to be actually in Form 5. Perhaps they had run out of exotic names. In the distance was the nirvana of the Sixth Form where rumour had it that boys could 'stay on' as long as they wanted. Indeed the massive Shanks Davies, the Head of Vikings, with his deep voice and receding hairline looked older than my dad. It was not unusual to see members of H.M. Forces striding across the quad as sixth formers, enlisted for National Service, before going to university to take up their Exhibitions (whatever they were). All of this served to underline how very, very insignificant we small boys were.

(Later research indicates that the use of these strange names for classes came directly from – where else – the Public Schools. 'Shell', was the apsidal end of the schoolroom at Winchester School, so called from its conch like shape. So the pupils who tenanted that room were The Shell. Shell was an intermediate between forms 3 and 4. The 'Remove' was used for the form between years 4 and 5 and used to be a class in which pupils spent an additional year to prepare for exams.)

As new bugs we were in no state to appreciate any of our surroundings because the fear of getting lost and of being late for the next lesson dominated. Eventually 'getting lost' became a standard excuse used by the artful, 'Sorry Sir, Got Lost'. So we were told that 'getting lost' was now a punishable offence, which made us more afraid of *really* getting lost. The other fear was losing your property, despite the help of Mr Cash and his nametapes and the issue by the school of a rubber stamp and inkpad with your convict number on it. Mine was 3358. In what I could only call a piece of mismanagement (or was it further torture), none of the first year intake had form rooms with personal desks. We used the Science and Chemistry lecture rooms and the Geography room. We were allocated blocks of lockers (for which you had to provide your own lock – tears being shed when keys were frequently lost), in the bowels of the school, aka 'The Bottom Corridor'.

These were blocks of 30 lockers standing vertically, the lids of which lifted up. Those of us who did not get a 'top locker', had to get our books etc. by ducking under the 'top locker' group and balancing the locker lids on our heads. What happened next was inevitable. Just as you were getting things sorted out at break, with locker lid poised on head, along would come a Prefect or similar sadist and, in passing, flip the lid up. The lid returned with a jolting impact to the back of your skull. The walls of the corridor echoed to the succession of yelps, which travelled from one end to the other. We became a little more circumspect about entering this 'theatre of cruelty', and tried to carry all our necessities for the day round in our overloaded school satchels. This led to the shedding of sundry kit as our little camel train struggled round the cloisters. (I must also comment on another wonderful recipe for chaos; at every change of lesson all the pupils changed rooms i.e. we went to the masters rather than they come to us. So every forty minutes herds of wildebeest surged in contrary directions down the corridors and cloisters. Educational madness?

We were allocated to our forms alphabetically by surname. I was in 3B. Boys in 3A always thought they were better than us, and 3C did actually morph into the form with the most head bangers and troublemakers. Life in 3B was hilarious, the hilarity arising from the relief that the poor little sod being picked on or duffed up wasn't you. Our form master, mainly for registration and notices, was a scientist called Watts. 'Sparky' probably had drawn the short straw or maybe it was his turn to have a first year class but he did not seem too enamoured by his role. His punishment for all boys who had failed to put a brown paper backing on their General Note Books (why for God's sake) was a whack on the behind with a retort stand – a nice scientific touch.

My natural questioning attitude, quickly brought me into confrontation with 'Sparky' in the 'class punishment incident'. For some reason 'Sparky' said he had to go to the staff room and demanded absolute silence in his absence. Exit Sparky, cue mayhem; books thrown; caps skimmed across room, boys trapped in the 'fume cupboard'. When Sparky returned he said he could hear the racket all the way downstairs and that as a punishment the whole class would do 100 lines. In a majestic and supremely foolish moment, only equal to the time when I volunteered to box the mighty Kenny Parr, the 'cock' of Windle Junior School, I stood up and said, 'I am sorry, I cannot do that Mr Watts.'

'Pardon?' said Sparky, 'and pray tell us, **Mr French**, why not?'

'Because I sat here in silence when you were out'

Sharp intake of communal breath, hisses from friends, enemies and enemies yet to be.

'Ah,' said Sparky, in his best sarcastic tone. '**You see, Master French**, this is a **form** punishment. You are a member of this **form** are you not, ergo, you are all punished as a **form**.' Well I did try to get justice for the common boy.

Form 3B turned out to be a nice middle of the road group. We did not have anybody ferociously brilliant like Ken Clarke, 3A, (not that Ken Clarke) or Bill Tunstall, 3C, who could probably solve quadratic equations in his head at the age of two, but we did not have any 'hard men' like Mickey Morris or Glynn Williams, (3C) who were to be avoided at all costs, especially when they were smiling. I once discovered that, when I grabbed a passing ankle in a rugby melee, upending its owner, the appendage belonged to none other than the said Williams. His retribution was swift. At the next scrum I felt my nose being squashed by his forearm. Kenny Booth had the right tactic to avoid such carnage. I can still see him running down the field with some assassins in pursuit and just throwing the ball away to avoid being tackled.

But, there was always an up side when these latter 'hard knocks' went into action against the thugees of the upper school. Indeed the slug fest between Morris (3C) and the fearsome 'Spike' Riley (Shell Alpha), egged on by a cheering mass, will forever be in my scrapbook of 'Great Fights' alongside Ali and Foreman. Spike was a tough cookie but unfortunate in that he had a very pronounced Roman nose, which the six-foot Morris was able to hit hard and often. Despite trading blow for blow, copious blood was flowing from Spike's conk, until he was saved by the (playground) bell. Sometime later the victorious Morris left the school dishonoured but not unsung.

At the end of every break an amazing lunacy overtook us. Access to the school was by two double doors at each end of the building – only one of which was ever opened. After keeping boys out of the school during break, the duty prefect would open the single door and wisely stand aside. A wall of humanity charged for the six by four foot opening and you just hoped that you would be carried safely along in the press of bodies up the stairs to the classrooms. You could also find yourself swept downstairs to the Bottom Corridor. In my first experience of this phenomenon, my new leather school satchel (double straps like a haversack, not a single strap girlie outfit) was torn off my back by an amiable cove called John Davies. Johnny, who as 'Sam Shed' later in life, found fame on *The Wheeltappers and Shunters Club* and *Coronation Street*, was also an excellent cartoonist and illustrator. He also to my astonishment first appeared on TV emerging from a gents toilet in Alan Bennett's play *Sunset across the Bay*. He was one of those boys who passed the eleven plus when nobody expected him to and, sad to say, he did not take to grammar school life. Anyway I belted him.

Just off the Bottom Corridor was the Junior Library. This rather scruffy room had in it a snooker table, a table tennis table and round the walls were the pictures of famous Cowley Rugby teams. I think there were some tatty books there also (it was a library!) But the real attraction of the JL was that it housed the school Tuck Shop. It was managed by 'Pam',(more of whom later), but the actual selling of confectionary was done by 'volunteers' i.e. us. It was a shambles, as you would expect. Boys on duty behind the counter were 'extremely generous' to friends on the other side, so a fair amount of goods were slid across the counter in exchange for rather small amounts of cash. There was no way that the business could have been run at a profit and I am sure that Pam must have made up the deficit out of his own pocket.

Every Friday afternoon the whole of year one (3A, B, C,) had a Swimming Lesson at the Municipal Baths in Boundary Road. This release from the confines of school was welcome but had its drawbacks. The afternoon timetable at Cowley was split into three forty minute periods. We discovered that our Form swimming time was 2 pm to 2.40 pm, and that we were supposed to make our own way down to the Baths in our lunchtime and then return to school, bedraggled and chlorinated, for the last period of the week, starting at 3.20pm. What an injustice. There was, as I remember, no convenient bus to take us back, and it was easier to trudge through Queen's Park and up the hill to school, fortified by a 'crisp butty' (barm cake stuffed with crisps) purchased from the shop opposite the Baths. To add insult to injury, 3C, who had their swimming lesson scheduled at 3.20 were allowed to walk down to the baths after the first taught period at 2.40 and go straight home after their session. My reward for this aquatic experience was my 25 yard Swimming Certificate, two widths of the pool. In spite of my pleas to the contrary, I was reminded by all and sundry, that I put my foot down on the return width so I was **cheating**! Wisely I kept my counsel and, like most alarums the crime faded into history.

Despite the fact the nation was emerging from the ravages of war, and many of austerity measures imposed by the Government were still in place, the purchase of School Uniform was undertaken with a competitive gusto by most families. As far as I recall the only 'compulsory' items of uniform were the maroon school cap, 'to be worn both to and from school', and the grey and maroon striped tie. Keith Farrington seemed to follow this to the letter. From the First to the Fifth year he seemed to wear the same suit with the school tie. But most of us, or rather our mothers, went for the full fig. Blue blazer with gryphon badge and motto '*Non Sibi Sed Omnibus*' (Not for one but for all'), grey short trousers, grey socks with two maroon circle tops, grey pullover with maroon V-neck, all could be purchased from Lawson's or Tyrer's (posh). Other ranks went to the Co-op, which latterly changed its name to the more snooty 'Helena House'. A new word in our vocabulary was *'barathea'*. This apparently was a top quality blazer material. I can't recall anyone I knew having one. The big debate centred around exactly when one could wear this apparel. Mum decided that I could not put my uniform on until the first day of the school term. Word on

My original old school badge

the street was that some of my mates were 'playing out' in their new kit and that one boy had actually gone on holiday in his. However, a couple of weeks before my first term, we went to the travelling exhibition of The Festival of Britain in Manchester and I am certain that I wore my new uniform then.

Uniform wars threatened to break out later in my school life when it was discovered that if you became a member of the First XI cricket team you could wear a maroon blazer. Mum was off to town like a shot but no maroon blazers were to be found. She extended her search to Liverpool, and came back with a maroon blazer. To my horror, this was a Girl's coat, with sewn in badge and buttons 'on the wrong side'. Such obstacles were minor challenges to Mum. She covered the original badge with my Cowley badge and switched the button holes round. However it was, shall we say, rather roomy in the chest department. 'No one will notice.' she said. Some one must have let the cat out of the bag, as I was ribbed by my mates about my possible pregnancy. To make matters worse, Brian Wilson's competitive mum got him a maroon blazer which he brazenly wore – and no one gave a monkey's. *Sic fatur Brianus lacrimans.*

Sweets were briefly taken off the ration, but due to excessive demand were quickly re-rationed (I well remember running to Bancroft's Shop only to see a 'sold out sign'.) To make matters worse, food rationing had ended in supposedly defeated Germany

Lawson's advertisement in the School Magazine

on 6 January 1950. Getting new ration books was a real pain as we would have to join a long queue at the distribution centre in Windle Pilkington School. So it was a relief to get 'Good Old Winnie' back in the government in October 1951, with 321 seats to 295, even though Labour polled far more *overall* votes than the Tories. (What a weird system.) I was always a Churchill supporter and could not understand why the country, which he had led to victory in THE WAR had just ditched him. My dad, a conscripted (over 30), reluctant soldier and Labour voter all his life, called him 'Old Dog Chops' and said he prolonged THE WAR to suit his purposes i.e. keep the Empire. My mother, a staunch Conservative, (all teachers then voted Conservative), raised a disapproving eyebrow. However there was no doubt that the returning soldiers, who had fought and won the War, had very little in common with a post war Churchill, and were not going to settle for a resumption of 'class rule'. They particularly resented the preferential treatment given to the 'officer class' – 'jumped up whipper snappers', according to my late father-in-law.

What of the Festival?

I was somewhat miffed when nearly all the buildings of the Festival of Britain were soon demolished, especially the Skylon, which I thought was great. Worse still, to discover that it was 'Good Old Winnie' who wanted to eradicate all remnants of the preceding Labour efforts, a feat he did manage, apart from the Royal Festival Hall, whose architecture was dire. (Perhaps that was Winnie's joke.) Most conservative minded figures were against the Festival, seeing it as a blatant move by the Government to buy votes and put on a final 'show' prior to the upcoming election. However true that may be, the Festival was educational, uplifting and a huge success.

'Britannia', symbol of the Festival of Britain

Barry Turner, the author of *Beacon for Change*, was a boy like myself in 1951. Coming from Bury St Edmonds he could actually get to the Festival itself, lucky dog. He was struck by the newness of everything and the startling colours, which were a relief from the drabness of post war Britain. The individual exhibits gave the message that modern science could be engaged as a servant of progress. He himself saw that education could be discovery. Most of all the Festival was to be fun and Herbert Morrison, for the government, wanted to 'hear the people sing'. And for five shillings admission they both sang and danced many nights away. A family friend who lived Nottingham used to travel down (or is it up?) to the Festival, particularly for the ballroom dancing under floodlights on the South Bank. The Nation was ready to move forward.

'The Skylon'

'The Dome of Discovery'

Turner's most exciting 'personal experience' however, came at the Bury St Edmonds schools' *Festival of Song and Dance*. A dire affair to be sure for a second year grammar school boy, dragooned into swelling the audience of proud parents.

'We were in the front row bored witless, until the finale when a girl of generous appurtenances demonstrated her handstands and cartwheels. Above a bare midriff she had on a frilly top secured by a ribbon round her waist and another ribbon tied at her neck. In mid act the ribbon snapped and when she went into her cartwheels her modesty, delectable beyond the wildest dreams of hormonally challenged teenagers, was revealed to all. Encouraged by our wild applause this true artist gave us an encore.'

(As a post script, the *Daily Telegraph* ran an article in January 2011 commemorating '60 years on' from The Festival, stating that my lovely Skylon was unceremoniously dumped into the River Lea. This prompted several readers' letters claiming to know of its 'true' end. *Either,* on being lowered, it was canibalised during the night by the public, *or* it lay in the garden of Jacko Moya, its designer, in Rye, *or* sheets of it were used to build a green house in Woodford Green. 'I suspect that very little of the Skylon will be found at the bottom of the River Lea', commented Emeritus Professor MMR Williams (22/1/2011). Well he should know he's an Emeritus!)

The world was turning out to be a strange place and stranger still, when we discovered that our former WWII 'comrades', The Russians and 'Good Old Uncle Joe' Stalin, were now our sworn enemies and that we were fighting a 'Cold War' against communism. The first skirmish in this 'non-war' was a very real, and very bloody war, in Korea where from 1950 to 1953 the communist backed North Korea and the U.S. backed South Korea attempted to annihilate each other. But 'the 39th Parallel' was far away from schoolboy consciousness, and who were these Koreans anyway? The one true memory I had of this time was a headline in a sort of satirical paper called *Billy's Weekly Liar,* which read, *'General MacArthur Flies Back To Front' (to keep the dust out of his eyes).* This was a one sheet 'rag' which suddenly appeared in school and until writing this book I never knew its origin. It was published by Bolton's of Preston and sold in Joke Shops for three pence. By the time it reached us it had gone through so many hands it was always falling apart.

Back at School

I t was a tradition at Cowley that caps should be worn on the left side of the head and as far back on the head as possible. I have no idea why this was so. Perhaps it was in imitation of army regiments which also had distinctive ways of wearing headgear, or perhaps it was to hide the cap altogether. We followed the tradition and were constantly adjusting the silly things. Many older and bolder souls took off their caps as soon as they were out of sight of the school gates. (Wearing a school cap at the age of 18 was a bit ridiculous, although I later was unable to persuade the current Headmaster of this logic. ('Thin end of the wedge, French.') A change in cap design altered the fashion. I think it was when I was in year two or three that a brighter version of the maroon 'titfer' appeared with a huge 'duck bill' peak. If you didn't feel daft before, you did now. You couldn't wear it on the back of the head because the peak reared up and made the wearer more conspicuous, and because of the size of the peak it didn't stuff into back pockets as easily. It did I suppose serve as good cricket cap. Maybe that was the main idea.

The rising star in our form was my namesake 'Big' French. I was obviously 'Little' French. He was to be none other than Ray French, now MBE, international rugby player at School and University level, going on to Senior Rugby Union and League, and commentator for the BBC, where he exchanged regular banter with Welsh international Johnathan Davis. 'Ah, yes, but, **Johnath-on, did 'ee touch it down, I don't think 'ee did**'. He also returned to be Head of English at Cowley and naturally Rugby Coach. In truth he is my second cousin, but I confess I have shamelessly used 'the family name' in exchanges round the globe on the lines of 'You're from St Helens?' 'Yes.' 'Rugby League eh?' 'Yes.' 'French?' 'Yes.' 'Any relation to Ray French?' 'Oh yes he's my brother/uncle/ granddad' – choose response to suit.

Ray was the mildest of boys and allowed our teasing, 'You can't really **play** rugby you're just big,' when he could have swatted us like flies. Indeed he did swat me by accident once when in a kick-about soccer game after the A level exams, I unleashed one of my 'killer' sliding tackles (take the man and ball) and woke up about ten feet away from him with little birds singing in my head. But I once took a fiendish delight in making him field at 'long on' at both ends of the ground in a match at Liverpool Institute – and he didn't much like cricket anyway. But when he hit the ball, it sure stayed hit

Earlier in our Cowley careers, I 'crossed swords' with Ray, so to speak, in a very boring English lesson. Ray and his sidekick Gordon 'Goller' Deakin were sitting directly behind me and, looking for some diversion during 'quiet reading', was poking a pencil in the back of my neck. It was not particularly harmful, just irksome, and I could feel myself getting to the breaking point. Suddenly I stood up, turned round and armed with my trusty rapier aka fountain pen, delivered two long slashes of the finest *Quink* blue ink across Ray's astonished face. It was a wonderful feeling and well worth the clip on the head from Lefty (Lees). I think he had seen what was going on and left me to it. There were no recriminations, no detentions – just silence.

Sport, or we should say Rugby Union was massive at Cowley. The school was a leading force in school rugby in the North West and several alumni had become full Internationals. In my time, Soccer was anathema and you were lucky to find a round ball anywhere on the premises. For an aspiring Grammar School, Rugby League was beyond the pale. Now I was a keen soccer player but just as eager to make the grade in any new sport, so I was ready to embrace the 15-man code. Unfortunately I found its embrace a little too 'hearty', shall we say. In our first games lesson I scored a try; just picked the ball up and jinked my way through. The Games master, Steve Harrison, who played at centre for St Helens Rugby League, called me over, and asked my name. To my mortification and those of my out jinked opponents, he then made us 'walk the move through' to demonstrate my 'side step'.

The upshot was that I found myself selected on the wing for the Under 12s versus Merchant Taylors', Liverpool. Proud I was, but pride goeth before ... MTs' kicked off and the ball sailed straight into my arms; a good catch. As I was debating which of my repertoire of skills to demonstrate next I was hit simultaneously by three hulking forwards and left for dead. Winded and bruised I can still hear Spike Reilly cackling, 'Use you weight Frenchie!' For the next seven years I used every trick in the book to avoid selection for school rugby; twisted ankle; cross-country match; fallen off my bike etc. In fact running a cross-country in winter at Manchester Grammar School in the pouring rain, *and* finishing last, was probably only a little less painful than being buried by Merchant Taylors'. My lack of 'beef' was a problem for Rugby. To try to call my bluff, I was occasionally appended to the team sheet for linesman's duties. Even this task was confusing. In soccer the linesman indicates the throw in by pointing his flag in the direction of the play, in rugby he points his flag back to the team who has won the line out.

The 'curse of Rugby' struck again sometime later when I dived in to ankle-tap 'Flossie Ingham', the school 100 yards record holder. All I remember was a sharp pain in the eye plus lots of blood, as the heel of Flying 'Flossie's boot made contact with my eye socket. I was quickly attended to by the referee, who after a cursory glance said, 'It's nothing much, just pop down to St Helens Hospital and have it stitched.' Nothing much! It was my bloody eye and there was no way I was having stitches. I rather thought a solicitor would be preferable. But as usual, a 'consultation' with Dad, who used to regale me with the tale of 'playing with blood coming out of his lace holes' and a quick dab of iodine, set the matter to rest.

In fact *size*, not intelligence or class was the real discriminator in school life. No one knew or even cared in what district anyone lived or whose father was director of this company or a doctor or academic. In fact when 'Sparky' went round the class in 3B asking what our father's did (not mothers, note!) there did not seem to be much in it between my dad (insurance agent for the 'Blackburn' and Len Kilshaw's dad (insurance agent for the 'Royal London') although we came to blows over it. I think I was in the Fifth form before I discovered that a lad named Davies was the son of the Managing Director of Beecham's Pills and (bigger shock) *had wine at dinner.* No, we were all clever, we had all 'passed', and the majority of us were the first children in the family to have a chance to do what our parents could not do. We were the cadre of 'working class' children who were to be the movers and shakers of the future. I cannot concur with left leaning authors that **all** working class families lived in terraces with a tin bath and an outside 'lav'. All the houses on the Haresfinch estate, newly built by Harris in 1939, and part private/part council owned, had indoor bathrooms and toilets. Tucker (2014) makes this supporting statement. *'By the end of our first day (at Cowley) it became plainly obvious that the teachers were totally disinterested in appearances and parents' economic standing and passionate only about the abilities of the kids"*

The real shock was the fact that some of our new colleagues, who were the same chronological age as us were, well, **men** to put it bluntly. These hairy men/boys, several of whom I had previously pursued in vain in the St Helens Junior School 100 Yards Final, dominated the rugby field and the athletics track, their deeper voices echoing through the showers in counterpoint to our treble chirpings. Some of the hairy ones had their own 'worries', which they covered by wearing swimming trunks in the showers. They were ordered to remove them by a succession of PE teachers whose mantra was 'You lot haven't got anything I haven't seen before'. (Very sensitive). However, these hairy men also knew more about 'the facts of life'; more of which anon.

The school attempted to remedy this imbalance by running teams based on weight/height criteria like 'The Bantams', which I think was under nine stone and five foot and 'The Colts'. I was able to play for the Bantams even in my fourth year, but fame refused to beckon. Just as I was anticipating pounding a few 11 year olds – the matches were cancelled. Now strange to relate, I was eventually selected for the School. At the ripe old age of

19, I played my one and only game for Cowley, in a Third Extra XV Rugby team, and I produced almost the same jinking run that I had performed so many years ago. With one defender left to beat, I passed the ball to Ricky Rawlinson who scored under the posts. He had the gall to claim credit for his unopposed try. I was content to show the Rugby world what it had lost.

The Staff

In Them Good Ol' Days, teachers were all described as 'characters' and I think I would testify to that. Most of our masters were First Class Honours Graduates, and in the main unencumbered by unnecessary teaching qualifications and the need to be accountable to anyone but God and The Headmaster. They taught the curriculum as they saw fit. And it was accepted by pupils and parents that the teachers were there to teach you academic disciplines. They were not there as pastoral guides, counsellors or facilitators. Parents' evenings were there so that staff could tell your parents what you were or were not doing, not an invitation for parents to tell the school what they thought it should be doing. Careers advice was there to tell you to go to University or College. Respecting teachers, elders and policemen was part of our parents' credo, and this was passed on to us. It was something that lasted, along with 'not showing us up' and 'not eating in the street', until the Sixties washed it all away. (In some cultures this deference still remains. I recall, with some affection, the guileless reply of a Karachi headteacher to my supposedly probing question;

"Where do your parents 'stand' in your education system?"

"Behind that gate."

Each teacher was king in his own classroom and developed his own 'act'. There was also a wide range of after school activities all run by the staff; Rugby practices, Chess Club, Junior Games Club, Debating Society, Drama Group etc. I must add here that all senior schools in St Helens usually put on a Christmas Play, but by far the outstanding event of the year was the Gilbert and Sullivan Opera put on by The Parr Central Secondary Modern Boys School, (motto *Omnia Perficere Potest)* with Robert Dorning (later a TV actor) in the lead role. Could this happen today? I think not.

From my own later teaching experience, eleven-year-old boys will often refer to you as 'Dad', followed by, 'Oh sorry Sir'. For us there were father figures, grandfather figures, big brother figures, both nice and nasty. There were also a few female teachers who were accorded great respect because they were women. We had to address them as 'ma'am'. Mrs Freeman was brilliant teacher and effortless disciplinarian. We never moved in her lessons. (She also knew my mum!)

On a lighter but very un-pc vein, a young female Geography teacher came to us when we were in the Shell Year two. She was a real honey and wore Jane Russell type sweaters. It was lust at first sight and we all looked forward to her patrolling the room, bending over you to check your pulse (sorry, work). One lesson she covered something about rift valleys and used the word 'undulating', which she explained as the rise and fall of hilly terrain. Our minds were put in overdrive about the rise and fall of her hilly terrain and so, it was decided that, in the next lesson, Kenny Booth would innocently ask her to explain again what 'undulating' meant when she came round to mark his book. This he did and to our great delight she smacked him round the head and put him in Detention. What larks, Pip.

Back to the Masters: The **grandfather figures** were Jock Stronach (French), 'Spud' Powell (Woodwork), real gentle, kindly men, 'Chinny' Evers (Music), a bit stricter, never let us bring our own music to class, 'Kipper' Addshead (Latin) probably the oldest man on the planet but a great teacher. He said he would pay my hospital bills if I ever had a breakdown through overwork, 'Tommy' Dawe (Maths), Sorry, Tommy, I just didn't get how two minuses ever made a plus, 'Fuzzy' Fairhurst (Art) 'I'm just popping downstairs'; Pop Handley, PE and RI, a miniature muscular Christian, 'Froggy' Frodsham (Chem); had the most hacking cough I had ever heard reputedly from a lung wound in the war and finally, 'Sarky' Heywood (Deputy Head/Chemistry), 'Sarky' was the grandfather I was glad I hadn't got. Did he really like teaching? Did he like anybody? (In my own professional experience, I found that all Deputy Heads were shall we say, 'quick to anger'.)

Father figures; 'Lefty' Lees (English), always gave me 7/10 for everything and had torn gown in which he tied knots to hit us with; 'Dan' Rodden (English and Drama) plus modest Battle of Britain pilot, 'Flash' Clifton (Latin), impeccable dresser, wealth allegedly coming from his wife's chemists shop, could be easily persuaded to talk about his tank command in WWII, Rugby fanatic; 'Smityed' Smith (History), taught us how to make proper notes and learn more about British Rail disasters, Paddy Moss (Maths), lovely man, i/c senior cricket, 'Basher' Bailey (English), a Lincolnshire Yellow Belly, never bashed anyone in his life, Joe Drane (History), 'one of the Lincolnshire Dranes', very good on the hegemony of the Baltic', 'Harry' Siggers (French), very funny, very rude and cultured, tried to deliver us from St Helens oikiness, 'Moggie' Mearns, (Physics) Brilliant! How did you get us through O level? George Tough (English), excellent, hilarious, made us like Milton, 'Big Bill' Brady (Geography), he actually wrote books! 'Ducky' Duckworth (Biology/Gen. Science) lived near me, so OK for lifts home on his motorbike (Not like *The History Boys!*)

Big Brothers: 'PAM' Philip Anthony Morley (French/Keeper of the Cricket Field), and just about everything else in my school life, 'Rocky' Rawsthorne (Maths), I started to enjoy maths, 'Bill' Boyd (Physical Education), turned P.E. round in the school versus Rugby interests, Ken Friar (History), great bloke could talk about anything to him, Ducky Groarke (French) a real leftie, thought I was on the far right of politics.

On the Dark Side: 'Doc' Smith, (Maths) a direct descendant of Wackford Squeers, could hit you equally hard, forehand or backhand, a terrifying prospect in full cry. Very frightening. We once thought he had killed George Hewitt, who was a chronic asthmatic, but a bit of a comedian. During a maths lesson the wind was blowing

PHILLIP ANTHONY MORLEY, B.A.

through one of the top windows and we asked that it be closed. The Doc got up on the desk and with his height closed the offending window. 'Ah,' said George, 'it's Sherpa Tensing'. Laughs all round; a nice topical joke. The Doc jumped down from the desk and gave George a massive blow to the head. George staggered back to his seat and we all froze. No one dare say anything. An awful incident, which we trust could not happen today.

Lost without trace; 'Billy' Bilinki (History), a Greek teacher with a wooden leg, a crutch and discipline problems? He was the victim of constant japes including one in which a leg of his chair was partially sawn through so that on sitting he, and chair, collapsed. Could do nothing to help. Sorry Bill, and lastly 'Shem' Webb (physics and RI) – of whom more later.

It is a truth, seemingly ignored in today's educational turmoil, that children, and boys in particular, need structure and a discipline administered by teachers who like children and like to teach. They do not need teachers as 'friends' or 'learning facilitators'. With every good teacher, you knew exactly where you stood and how far you could go and that I aver will always obtain.

Early setbacks

M y early days at Cowley were, sad to say, not of the sunniest. Truth to tell, I was fairly worried most of the time. Not only was the whole business a massive upheaval for me, but I was a perfectionist who wanted to do my best, but against whom the fates seemed to conspire. My opening gaffe was in an essay on '*St Helens, My Town*'. I wrote about Beecham's Pills, as did we all, and continued to say that the name Beecham is revered, as it is the name of the conductor of the Halle Orchestra ... Sir John Barbarolli!

Lefty Lees nearly died laughing. Wrong conductor, wrong orchestra! At least he said I knew two classical conductors. Such shame!

Just two weeks into the term, I was sent to Cantle to be caned! The indignity and humiliation; could I ever hold my head up in polite society again? We were playing rugby one afternoon when an emissary from the Head came with a message, 'The following boys to get changed and report to Mr Cantle's office.' I was on the list of about 10 boys. Mystified, we all trooped to the changing rooms and then went to collect our school satchels which had disappeared from where we had thrown them – on top of our lockers, while we ran off to the changing rooms (which incidentally were later used as background in the film *Chariots of Fire*). Then it dawned on us that somewhere in the haze of morning assembly, which to us was now light years ago, we had been told, 'for the last time', not to leave our property lying about on the top of our lockers. Oh Bugger! Off we went up to Cantle's office and he was waiting there for us with our bags. 'Ah, (pause) you have no doubt come for your possessions, gentlemen?' he said. 'Yes Sir.' 'You will of course (pause) have to pay.' Then little Alan Birchall, the darling of our crew, asked in all innocence, 'How much Sir?' Cantle, smiling like Sher Khan the tiger, said, 'Come inside and find out.' One stroke of the cane across the seat of our pants. Well it could have been worse. We could have been still wearing shorts.

I was by now imagining an exciting future scenario envisioning my dad, who had sorted out a few bullies in his time and had been a schoolboy boxer to boot, walking purposefully into the school, parting the masses before him, grabbing a pleading Cantle with one hand and giving him a good thrashing with the other. So, on arriving home, I eagerly showed off the welt prominent on my tender backside. He looked up from his paper, asked about the incident and said, 'Well, you won't do it again will you?' What a betrayal. Let down by your own flesh and blood. The world was suddenly a darker place – until my mates called round to play football.

The next tragedy to occur was the FAILURE OF THE FRENCH VERB TEST. I had started off very brightly in French. My ace in the hole was that my mother had done French and so could be of help. For our first homework from the (then) fearsome 'PAM' Morley, we had to learn the conjugation of the verb 'etre' for a test the following day. Piece of cake. I recited 'je suis, tu es' ... to mum and she corrected my pronunciation until I was word perfect. Came the test and I looked forward with confidence to a 100% pass. 'OK, 3B, now write down the conjugation of the verb etre in French and English.' Ah, did he say **write**? I thought French was a spoken language. How unfair can this life get. With swimming brain I could just about remember how to spell, 'Je suis' and the rest was lost in the panic. I got 1/10 and all failures had to write the conjugation out 50 times.

Again I demanded justice. I explained to PAM, as simply as I could, that as French was a spoken language we should have been tested on the pronunciation. I even tripped off the whole verb. No dice; 'I asked you to write it not say it. Collect your impot paper at break.' Suicide was now a distinct possibility. But a 'mystery' illness in the next period (Music) might get me sent home early, and give me an afternoon to write his damn verbs. And that is what transpired, plus a dose of womanly sympathy from the School Secretary, (who later married Ally 'Bill' Boyd the PE Master).

I was learning how to survive

I was rather shocked to discover that the sadistic 'PAM', who had become Public Enemy No 1, was not only in charge of Junior Rugby and Cricket, but also put on trips to France (£32.00), holidays in Wales at Abergele (£5), and ran something called the Junior Games Club. This took place after school from 6.30 to 8.30 in the Gymnasium and we played 'Pirates' with all the gym apparatus and the suicidal/homicidal 'Murder Ball'. The object of this team game was to get a heavy 'medicine ball' onto your opponents mat at the other end of the gym while they tried their combined best to kill you. Some bloody noses and broken wall bars, but amazingly no fatalities. As we went back to school for Junior Games Club, we would, in summer, go on our bikes and then there was the opportunity to flout holy writ i.e. to ride your bike across the polished hall and if you were really daring across the upper balcony. Next morning, in Assembly, we used to point out to 'unbelievers' the tracks of our tyres.

In winter we went back to JGC on the bus. One evening one of our group, Eddie Duncan, a lovely lad and a born joker, suggested we go in to a coffee bar or some such for a drink before we got our bus home. So the four of us, me, Eddie, Brian Wilson and Kenny Booth all piled in to some dive in Claughton Street. Now I don't know why but I seemed to be the only one who ordered a drink, tea, as it happened. Then Eddie pulled his masterstroke. One of our Masters, 'Lefty' Lees, would respond to any boy who had the temerity to ask to go to the toilet with the phrase, 'I'll slap you down, smelly'. That was quite funny, but it became hysterical when purposefully repeated by Eddie, and I had a mouthful of tea. I struggled to contain the draught but to no avail and a stream of tea fountained into the air and across the table. We made our excuses and left.

Then the guilt set in. By tomorrow someone sitting in that café would have reported this incident to Cantle. After all we had our uniforms on, clearly showing we were Cowley boys. It would be announced in assembly with Cantle's usual gravitas. Maybe I would be expelled. A restless night and a brave face the following

29

morning. Assembly came and thankfully went. But what about if the person who had seen me hadn't yet reported it? After a few more assemblies, I realised that people didn't care two hoots about little boy's behaviour and I was home and dry.

So bit by bit I gradually learned the ropes and by the summer of that first year I had my first bit of 'recognition' as a cricketer. Cowley's summer sport was cricket with wickets prepared by a groundsman and real leather seamed balls for matches. I was a fast bowler and if I pitched the ball up batsmen seemed to miss them. We had matches against Hutton Grammar, Ormskirk, Upholland, Prescot, all umpired by 'Pam' who picked the team, and by now had been transformed in my mind from bastard to saint. One thing always impressed me and that was the posting

Cowley Ist Year Cricket Team
back row; Kilshaw. Leigh, French, Lee, Barett, Tunstall, Birchall
        (Scorer)
front row; Lawrenson, Heath, Dixon, P.A.Morley, Giliker,
        McCollum, ??

of the team sheet on the Quadrangle notice board. This was no bit of paper with names scribbled on it. This was quality vellum with the school crest, gryphon rampant, at the head, and space for all the team below, time of play, where to meet etc. Strange the things one remembers. The big 'kick' was that if you played an away game, one of you got to take the kit home overnight. This chore was looked on as a great privilege, being trusted with bats, balls, pads, stumps and the 'box', a pink plastic guard which we all wore to protect our, as yet, undescended testicles. (In a later episode, I remember Bill Tunstall having a lot of fun introducing the 'box' to the girls of Wade Deacon Grammar School – but I digress.)

The old '55' at her stand on the Town Hall Square

One painful/hilarious incident occurred when we were coming back by coach from some away game. I asked to be dropped off at the Town Hall Square, from which the '55' bus to Carr Mill departed. As we came into the square I could see the '55' ready to leave, so as the coach rolled to a stop, I opened the sliding door ready to leap out. Sliding doors slide both ways, and as the coach halted the door slid back and trapped my neck, so was stuck half in and half out of the coach. As I fought to get the door back off my neck, I was aware of the gales of laughter coming from my 'concerned' teammates. On the academic side I did well in the end of year exams and was placed in Shell A for the year 1952-3.

The Groves
of Academe (Shell A)

L ife in the second year meant two things a) you were
no longer in year one and more or less bully proof, although
in truth I was never bullied; b) you did Latin. (Latin
came to dominate my life to such an extent that I 'read Latin'
at University – sounds good, and I must say it has impressed
many. But why I chose to study a subject for three years that I did
not *really* enjoy I still cannot explain. I was good at it and,
I suppose, that was the pragmatic clincher.) Latin was good fun
because you could chant the conjugations and declensions
'amoamasamatamamusamatisamant' and there was more chance
for 'smut'. The accusative case of 'omnibus was 'omni**bum**', the
verb 'fero' (to carry) went fero, fers, **fert**, mitto,(to send) mitto,
mittis, **mittit,** the word for a scabbard was **vagina,** and anybody
picked to decline duco (to lead) was guaranteed a silent ovation
if he could get to the dreaded du**cunt** without hesitation.

However, in all seriousness, the beauty of Latin was, and still
is, that it gave you insight into the English language and other
European tongues (French, Italian, Spanish) and this I found
fascinating. Thus 'trivial' – of little importance – was derived from
trivia, a meeting of three roads. Romans didn't have cross roads
apparently and trivia or gossip was what they did at the trivia.
'Sincere' was derived from *sine cera* without wax. Roman
furniture makers would rub wax, cera, into the wood in order to
make it seem weathered. Thus wood without wax treatment,
sine cera, was true wood i.e. sincere. Some words came into being
as direct Latin words. '*Tandem*' the two-person cycle came from
the Latin *tandem* 'at length'. It was dubbed a tandem by some
lettered chap who, on seeing the prototype machine called it an
'at lengther'.

It was George Orwell who said that the only way to learn
Latin well was to have it beaten into you. (*Such were the joys;*

Narrative Essays). Now while I can assure readers that nothing like that happened, there was a certain fear in the room when 'Flash' Clifton was patrolling the desks. 'Flash' had a wonderful instrument to bring instant attention from the most recalcitrant pupil, his *'John Willy Persuader'*. This was the short spill off an old chair, which he kept in his desk and produced it from time to time during vocabulary tests which he would bring down on the knuckles of the laggard. He also employed a magnificent device for getting a boy to his feet, gently getting hold of his sideburns and lifting. The pain was irresistible. If you stood up it stopped. (I think it was called The Cumberland Creep in the Nigel Molesworth book, *Down with Skule*. As any fule kno.)

Two topics, however, could be assured to take this martinet from his chosen Latin *via*. One, was to open a discussion about the benefits of Rugby League over Union. We were all ardent St Helens (Saints) fans. Many of the moves that we tried on the school rugby pitches were first observed at Knowsley Road (alas no more) where first Duggie Greenall and Alan Prescott and later Vince Karelius and the peerless Tom Van Vollenhoven held sway. In time, of course, would come our 'old boys' Ray French, Ken Large, Geoff Pimblett. Flash would have none of this and counter attacked by alluding to the monetary greed of the players. 'You don't think these players enjoy the game do you? You can see the ££££ signs in their eyes every time they score'. The amateur versus professional debate could take up a good whack of 'Double Latin'.

During a 'wet games afternoon' he once showed us a film of supposedly 'the finest try ever scored in an international game'. This was the one scored by Prince Alexander Obolensky in 1936 for England versus New Zealand. We were underwhelmed. Unlike our glorious Rugby League, where the defence and attack are never too far from each other, the nippy aristocrat was given acres of space to sprint through the leaden defenders. 'Weren't New Zealand allowed to tackle him, Sir, coz he was a prince?'

A second temptation we laid for him was to 'get him on THE WAR'. I never did find out exactly what rank 'Flash' held but we knew he was 'in Tanks' and had an encyclopaedic knowledge of

That's what you call a try! Tommy 'Voll' scores, leaving his opponents on their knees.

the Ardennes. A place where the Germans were not supposed to be able to cross but did. The board was soon covered in arrows of attack, outflanking movements and German breakouts. Had 'Flash' been in charge the war would indeed have been over by Christmas.

In Year Two, 'Spud' Powell (Woodwork) was our form teacher, and for registration we sat on the woodwork benches. In the actual subject we had graduated from making models out of cardboard (first year) to actual wood with very, very sharp tools as was quickly evident when George Hewitt stabbed Peggy Loughran in the hand with a wood chisel. It may have been the other way round but it was a wood chisel and there was blood. I liked woodwork, all the shavings flying about, freedom to move about the workshop and the smell and feel of the virgin timber. I wasn't very accurate with my measurement and my planning left a lot to be desired but I produced a passable tool rack, which was given pride of place in Dad's shed. The problem with 'Woody' (as with Art) was that while it was good fun, what good was it going to be for YOUR FUTURE? At the end of Year Two we had to make choices of the subjects we would 'drop' in order to start the long slog to O levels, which we were always told were just a round the corner. So I dropped both Woodwork and Art and just thanked God that I did not have to take Chemistry with 'Sarky'.

However one subject which was compulsory along with Maths (why oh why?) was Physics. Now I quite enjoyed General Science with 'Sparky', but Physics was something else. Not only did we have complicated maths to do to calculate the coefficient of linear expansion, which seemed vital for the future of mankind but our teacher was 'Shem'. Clever children respond positively to positive teaching. They go ape in the presence of poor teaching. Mr Webb nicknamed 'Shem', as with his close-cropped white hair he looked like a biblical prophet *and* he taught us Religious Instruction, ('Go on, ask him what adultery means'.) was a hopeless disciplinarian.

Protected by an almost serene aura, he sailed through the chaos of Double Physics. 'Gather round the fwont boys', heralded the usual opening skirmish for places next to his bench for the demonstration of Newton's Trolly, which couldn't half travel if pushed hard enough. These places at the front bench were keenly fought over, not out of any interest in the subject itself, but simply out of self-preservation. The further you were away from the front the more likely it was that you would be wizzed to the back by two thugees to have your penis measured or Iceland Spar stuffed down your trousers. Yes, folks, sex had arrived. While I was fortunate never to be a victim of 'The Press Gang' I have, thanks to Physics, seen some 'todgers' which were unbelievably large for small boys. (So not only was I on the small side for Rugby, I didn't have a big one either – ignominy.)

The Physics Exam to split us in to Sets One and Two was a time for hysteria, panic and more hysteria. Only certain divinely inspired boys who just 'got' Physics, got anything like a good mark. One boy, called I think Shepherd, got something like 89%, someone else got 55% and then came the rest of us crowding the places between 20% and 0%. It was just ludicrous. I got into Set One (crème de la crème) with a marvellous 18%. Fortunately salvation was at hand in the shape of a new member of staff 'Moggie' Mearns, who in Year Three, quietly got us back on track and pushed us all through O level.

One of the features of the Physics textbook was that the answers to each problem set at the end of the chapter were given in the back of the book. When I was stuck with some intractable problem (most of my Physics homework fell into this category) my mother, 'She-who-never-gave-up-on-anything', would say 'Let's have a look at the answer'. Then taking the figures given in the question she would launch herself into furious computation to arrive at the answer in the textbook. I would produce the homework with mother's signature on it. 'Amazing work', said Moggie, 'Totally wrong of course'. Well we both tried.

However I must return to the chaos of Year Two Physics and the fantastic 'Door Bell Experiment.' One afternoon we arrived for our usual Double with 'Shem' to find the benches laid out in a square with electrical wire, solenoids, rheostats the works. For some reason there were two Forms put together to watch the demonstration of how a door bell works. Some of us had to stand on chairs to see. 'Shem' carefully explained the circuitry and how the connections were made, the current passed and thus, 'When I pwess this button the bell will wing' ... Silence; Giggles from watching horde; 'Mmm. I'll just check the contacts ... No they're fine ... twy again.' Silence. Suggestions were now offered from the spectators, 'I've got a penny, sir, it may be the meter'. (laughter) 'Could be the fuse gone in the plug?' 'Shem' checked the plug. It was fine. The button was again pwessed, again silence. The stifled mirth that came from one particular section of the room indicated, even to 'Shem', that mischief was afoot. 'Stand back from the expewiment', he commanded.

There, lying across the circuit was a small penknife, short circuiting the current and ruining the experiment. Every time the button was pushed the culprit put his knife across the wires. The offender was a boy called 'Ben' Large, better known in later life as Ken Large, centre threequarter for St Helens RL, Wembley try scorer and Cup winner. Then he was on the receiving end of 'Shem's right hand, the only time I ever saw him lose his temper, and a subsequent visit to the Head for a caning.

'Ben' had form as a bit of a lad, but the opportunity for devilment offered itself to both high and low. In a later time, boy wonder, Bill Tunstall (Cambridge Univ. and Senior Wrangler) mixed up some nitrogen triiodide in the Chemistry lab. As any 'fule kno', this substance is highly volatile and if you can find some innocent to bash it with a ruler it will explode. A fall guy was found, the deed done, and the resulting explosion brought staff running from all parts of the building. Rumour spread that Bill would be expelled. Most of us cynics doubted that. He was a 'premier league' brain and they had inbuilt 'political' protection.

So, who's got a Tele?

Owning a television set in the early 1950's was virtually impossible for most of our families, but *getting access to a television set by any means possible* was the next best thing and much Machiavellian planning went into this. Now, who do I know who has a tele? The man who lived next door to my grandma and who delivered our coal had one. Mr Fisher was a gift because he **wanted** to show off his new acquisition, a 'console' TV, a television set with a wooden sliding door which when closed made it look like a bookcase. Thus it was that I watched my first Cup Final (Arsenal 2 Liverpool 0) on his eight inch black and white screen. I should say I watched two Cup Finals at the same time. The transmission was then relayed from Sutton Coldfield and by some quirk of 'interference', the screen was split into two halves, both showing the same match i.e. two sets of goals, two Jimmy Logies scoring two goals, twice.

The Cup Final of 1953 was a **must** for any TV addict i.e. normal boy. It was Stanley Matthews' last chance of a winner's medal. So where could we go? The grapevine had it that someone next to Greenall's in Allan Road had one, and Kenny Greenall said he was going there to watch it. After some bribery, Kenny said he would ask his mum, if she would ask the next door neighbour if a couple of 'well behaved friends' could come round. Success! We witnessed what was possibly the most magical match ever played. Bolton, 3-1 up at half time, defeated 4-3 by a Mortensen hat trick and the influence of 'the wizard of dribble' who laid on the crucial pass for Bill Perry to crack in the winning goal. Strange that it was always known as 'the Matthews Final' when it was Morty that got the goals.

Laffak Field (a corruption of La Fough) was our playground. There was a natural spring of fresh water for thirsty boys. It had a copse (good for hide and seek), a huge pylon (good for forbidden climbing, and broken limbs in falling off), a full size soccer pitch (home of Haresfinch Rovers), a lake (frozen in winter), and direct access to the 'Burgy', a unique St Helens feature. The 'Burgy' was the spoil (sand deposit) from Pilkington's Glass Works. It spread for miles and many a brave lad was sucked down in it (well, it sounded good). From the field a path ran alongside the Liverpool – Wigan railway, which offered us a short cut home. We were absolutely forbidden to cross the railway lines, and so, naturally, we did. It must be added that to get to the field from our Crescent was about half a mile, and half a mile return. So two separate visits to the field was two miles, and that was before any activity. No wonder we were fit.

Like almost all children in the post war era, most of our leisure time was spent 'playing out'. Only rain would keep us inside. All the excitement was 'out there' be it in the woods, fields or just in the street. To go out after tea (evening meal) especially as winter darkness fell, was a thrill in itself. With the gaslight pole as a 'den' we played team hide and seek or 'Rally' in St Helens speak. If you were 'caught' you would be taken to the 'den', but if one of your 'free' men could escape capture and touch the 'den' then you were all free. Most of the hiding places were in 'forbidden' areas i.e. people's gardens or passage-ways (entrys). It is still strange to walk, today, over fields where there is not a child to be seen even on the brightest of afternoons. (Compare this with India where the maidans are packed with cricketers playing multiple matches.) I would also add that to my certain knowledge obesity, as a 'disease', was unknown. We were all generally normal i.e. thin. I can only remember one huge boy, the son of the grocer, who happily went by the name of 'Fat' Stratton. (His advantage was that he could swim in the coldest of waters, while we shivered on the edge.)

On 'Test Match' Saturday, August 15, we had drawn a complete televisual blank. England was on the verge of winning back 'The Ashes' from Australia, but we couldn't find a Tele. Fate, in the form of a young housewife from four doors down, took a hand. She came up to as we sat at the kerbside and said, 'I think we are going to win. Come in and watch the final overs'. So eight excited little boys saw Dennis 'Brylcreem' Compton strike the winning four, seated in front of a TV set at 113, Litherland Crescent. And, in a subtle reverse of the film hero who saves the day and then rides on, 'We never knew her name'.

Radio fun

With TV beyond our reach, Radio was available to all. The BBC's 'Light', 'Home' and 'Third' Programmes, were designed to cover all tastes. (I can't remember ever having the Third Programme on in the house. Who would want to listen to boring classical concerts? Now *Semprini Serenade* was 'proper' music) Entertainment was what we required, and I was brought up on a diet of *Paul Temple* and *Dick Barton* episodes. Many a tear was shed when 'Dick', 'Snowy' and 'Jock' solved their last case in 1951 and the exciting theme tune *Devil's Gallop* was heard no more. But then along came '*Journeyyyy ... intoooo...SPACE*', and we moved on with new heroes Jet, Doc, Mitch and Lemmey. (*Journey into Space* was produced by Charles Chilton, a fantastically talented writer who left school at 14 and got a job at the 'new' BBC after chatting to the commissionaire on the door.)

Simply put, BBC radio brought laughter into our lives. Almost every evening there was a half hour comedy show be it with Tommy Handley, Arthur Askey, Ted Ray, or Charlie Chester. Peter Brough, not a particularly good ventriloquist, brought his boy stage dummy, 'Archie Andrews' along and made a mint with 'Educating Archie'. Scores of top comedians filled the role of 'Archie's teacher' and one in particular was to become, for us, the funniest comic of all, Tony Hancock. '*H...H...Hancock's Half Hour*', with Dick Bentley, Sid James, Hattie Jacques and Kenneth Williams was said by 'the literati' to sum up *the British post war malaise*. Anthony St John Aloysius Hancock just made us laugh and every script was instantly committed to memory, to be replayed over again in the school playground. (We all had an amazing facility for remembering 'rubbish' which latterly has won many a Pub Quiz and Crossword competition) *The Goon Show* (Sellers, Milligan, Secombe and Bentine) was 'complete rubbish' to most adults. But the silly voices and catch phrases *'you've deaded me'* became part of our argot and if it was good enough for Prince Charles then it was good enough for us.

One of the longest running programmes was *The Archers*. This country story, which is still with us, had a huge following. For us its favourite voice was that of Old Walter Gabriel, *'well me old pal, me old beauty'*. This was spoofed by Tony Hancock in *The Bowmans* in which Hancock took the 'Old Walter' part of Joshua Merriweather, who was such a bad actor that it was decided to kill him off. But Joshua refused 'to die' and, due to his high audience rating, the BBC was forced to bring him back as Joshua's half brother. In this new persona, Hancock writes a new script and all the villagers fall down a disused mine shaft leaving the field clear for a family of new Merriweathers to take over, all played by Hancock of course.

Knowledge for the growing boy

The above was the title of a book, which I never actually saw, but which 'Rog' Dixon, our Form Captain, said he had read, which told you the 'facts of life'.(The pamphlet was by Sid G. Hedges, a devout Christian, and cost sixpence. published in 1941.) Now as someone who believed in Santa Claus when I was six,– a belief dispelled by Eddie Duncan on the school bus, 'It's your **dad,** you idiot.'– I was a bit slow on the uptake when it came to life's mysteries. Indeed when I was nine or ten, I confess I was puzzled by the frisson aroused by the production of something called '*Evening Nudes*' at the Theatre Royal. As my mate Brian Wilson tried to explain,' It's '*Evening Nudes*' from '*Evening News*' – it's a pun'. So it might have been, but as I had no idea what the word 'nude' meant it was lost on me. That did not stop me passing the Theatre (more than once) and having a long look at the promotional pictures. (Wow! I get it now!)

So back to 'Rog' and his worldly wisdom. 'Rog', who was one of the dark, hairy men/boys, read out from this pamphlet that, 'if a boy's erect penile member is rubbed vigorously, a sensational feeling will occur'. With that interesting piece of information, it was obvious that this thesis should be tested in vivo. So it was home to tea and a nice warm bath and YESSSS! it was truly sensational. (As every sentient male on this planet would testify 'orgasm' and scoring a goal are the nearest thing one ever comes to heaven.). From that time on, I, and every classmate, inhabited a different world, and like all would be Columbuses, we believed that we alone were the discoverers of this surprising and compulsive power. We became avid 'players of the pink oboe' as the comedian Peter Cook had it. Maybe that was where the guilt came from?

We were not helped by the fact that in all our families without exception, no one talked about sexual development. This total adult silence concerning all things sexual was weird, especially after the apparent sexual freedom, which we are told, occurred during the War. While I could probably understand my parents' reticence, (they were Baptists and almost any enjoyable human activity was 'sinful'), even the non-religious (C of E) parents said nothing to their offspring. It was really quite bizarre that the onset of normal human sexual activity should be treated with such complete 'omerta'. We just talked and talked, 'Do you think your dad wanks?' 'How gross.' 'Do you really think you can go blind?' 'Nah.' 'How many times can you do it in one session?' 'Mind your own business.' 'Does anything come out of the end yet?' 'Should it?' 'What's a Johnny Bag? 'Don't footballers wear them?' 'That a Jock Strap you twerp.'

And so, in this seemingly national rejection of the phenomenon, our debates raged on. At some time, exhausted both metaphorically and literally by our efforts, there seemed to be a consensus that '**not** doing **IT**' was 'a good thing' as apparently a chap called Onan had done it in the Bible and got himself smitten. So, lying through our teeth, we kept a clandestine class record of how many days it had been since our last 'deed'. Days and weeks were recorded, all false of course, and the trick was to get some unfortunate to confide in you that he had actually 'had one' and then announce to all the class that 'X is a wanker.'

A very mild version of pornography, advanced our education, which continued apace with the wondrous girls of 'Spick and Span', 'Razzle' and 'Tit Bits'. No one questioned why these well built girls were balancing on tree branches in bras and suspenders. It was 'common knowledge' that one of our classmates had the magazine delivered to his house. Generally objects of our attention (lust) were 'proper women', that is to say large ones. Film icons like Marilyn Monroe, Gina Lollothingibob, Sophia Loren and (our very own) Diana Dors were generously endowed. What would we have made of 'Twiggy' or Kate Moss?

'Health and Efficiency' was **the** notorious nudie magazine, but again, we found it extremely difficult to understand exactly

Is this pornography? You must be joking!

how these ample girls playing volley ball engaged in sex, as they did not have any signs of sexuality below the waist. A forerunner of the airbrush had been skilfully applied, but we, who had seen girl babies being bathed, worked out, using the erroneous logic of the naïve, that the vagina must move sort of downwards and backwards as women mature. Boys who had elder sisters knew everything however, and kept us up to date. Indeed it was from 'hot' stories typed on school paper, which made their way 'up the hill' from the Cowley **Girls** School, would you believe, that we furthered our knowledge of sexual congress in pretty well all its forms, although the homo/lesbian tendancy was still unknown to us.

As Barbara Menzies (1997) testifies, Cowley Girls were given a brief lesson on '*The Facts of Life*' but, as she recalls, the only thing she remembers, after being reassured about 'periods', was that you had to be married to have a baby. She wondered if, when the married couple knelt at the altar, a sort of divine baby making aura was sent down to them, but she was certain that a woman who worked for her mother had a son and she had never married. Total confusion on all fronts. This revulsion at our own development, and the rather strange activities of our contemporaries appears in several accounts.

Michelle Hanson (2012) growing up in leafy Ruslip, was an attendee at Haberdashers Secondary School. She did not like the interest in playing 'Doctors and Nurses' as a young girl, and was disgusted, in a thrilling way, to hear reports of the activities of her classmates who were it seemed delighted to 'reveal all' at various parties attended of course by boys. All these girls had breasts and wore brassieres. Michelle did not want breasts which wobbled about nor did she want 'periods' which came next. She was revolted at the sight of her vagina (she only saw it once) and was aghast at the whole idea of 'making babies'.

If you were a Catholic, things were a bit worse, as you were taught by nuns and priests who would brainwash you into celibacy? Brendan O' Neil (2014) gives the lie to that assumption. Educated by Catholics from the age of three to eighteen, he argues that the religious aura actually increased the fires of revolt;-

'You couldn't open a school bible without seeing the apostles with speech bubbles emerging from their heads saying, 'I'm Gay' or see a penis attached to the image of Christ. Some of us beheaded the little statues of St Vincent de Paul and the Virgin Mary. The classic graffiti found in the boy's toilets ran thus;

Wanking is evil
Evil is a sin
Sins are forgiven
So get stuck in

How on earth any of us emerged from this confusion to become the healthy, well-balanced adults we are today is a mystery (This should be read ironically).

One thing stood out in this period of burgeoning sexuality and that was the change in the gang's attitude to playing casual games of soccer. In prepubescent times, there could be twenty of us who would pick sides and play for a whole morning on Laffack Field no matter what your ability was. Gradually, more of our mates either did not want to play any more or 'mooched off' after about half an hour and just sat on the field talking and 'messing about'. One of the chief beneficiaries of this restless state was a well-endowed maiden who went by the name of 'Titty' Taylor and who, for a negotiable fee, would allow any goggle eyed youth to look at or feel her magnificent orbs – or so I was informed by the cognoscenti.

Speech Day and the school song fiasco

The annual Speech Day was the high point of the School year. It was the nearest that the school could get to being the Public School to which it aspired. It was for us juniors an awesome occasion. Programmes were published detailing all the school's examination successes, all the scholarships, which had been awarded to the boys going to University, and all the many Degrees and citations won by former students. All the masters wore their gowns, with capes of varying hues and they processed into the hall to take their seats on the stage, which was decked with flowers and plants. It looked like carnival time. Some of them, (the masters not the plants), looked quite presentable. The front half of the hall was reserved for parents and former students, so the school was distributed in the rear of the hall and on both sides of the balcony. For this occasion we were seated in form groups. The address was given by some worthy or other. I can't remember anything about their speeches except someone whose mantra was, 'It's all part and parcel of the Trade Union Movement'. Yes, it was bum numbingly boring, but help was always at hand in the form of 'Smityed', Mr Smith (History), who, taking pity on our plight, would issue us with back copies of the 'Trains Illustrated', stored in his cupboard. They fitted snugly inside the opened Speech Day Programme.

Speech Day always closed with the School Song, 'Cowley'. This song was written and composed by Chinny Evers (Music) and I must say it is a cracker as school songs go. I have never forgotten it. Its confident introduction and its pitch suitable for male voices high or low;

'In our work and in our leisure
May we help the school's good name
Seeking not a selfish pleasure

Seeking not a selfish fame.
But by doing all things well
Fearing not the truth to tell
We may help the school to swell
The name of Cowley'

There were two more verses on the same lines preaching incredible right – on guff, which can be found inside the back cover of this book.

Of course we bowdlerised the whole song, so that the second verse which begins:-

Other boys have gone before us
And have left their marks behind
became *And have left with marked behinds*

Every Speech Day was preceded by a rehearsal in the morning (more time off lessons). On this particular Speech Day we had taken our places on the balcony and observed 'Pam' Morley doing his MC bit in the hall below. All went well and just before lunch we arrived at the school song. (At this point I must digress to say that in the Hit Parade of the time the Number 1. record was *'The Mambo'*, *'Everyone's doin' it now'* as the song said. The mambo rhythm had a peculiar beat in which there was a pause at the end of each verse which was filled in by the band's shout thus;-

'Everyone's doin' it now (pause) **OOOOO!** (shout)

So 'Chinny' starts the introit to 'Cowley':-
(Piano) dum, didi dum dum dum di dum
dum dum dum, (louder) DUM DUM DUM – pause;-

The pause was filled by a huge shout of '**OOOO!**' from the assembled 4th and 5th years. Laughter all round even from attendant staff. 'Pam' went mad, 'Sabotaging the rehearsal'. Of course we all hoped that they would do it again on Speech Day proper.

But even the hard men of the Upper School had some decorum.

Literary pursuits
(comics)

From the time I started at Cowley, I must confess that I never read a 'proper' book again until I discovered James Bond in 1956. Books were what you **had** to read at school, and anyone who has been forced to read *Guy* (Sodding) *Mannering* as a form reader, doled out to us with glee by 'Lefty' Lees, will attest to a distinct decline in enthusiasm for the classic works. Now comics were a different matter. As avid readers of all things trivial we devoured them. I must point out that we prided ourselves on **not** reading picture comics. We had graduated from the *Beano* and *Dandy* many moons ago and, let's face it, people who bought picture comics were the types that read aloud, followed the words with their fingers and dribbled. Our Comics were the BIG FOUR, *Wizard* and *Adventure* on Tuesdays and *Rover* and *Hotspur* on Thursdays. These were well written stories of 'derring do' be it on the sports field, in the jungle or the battle front. (I always had to make sure I hid the current copy to stop mum pinching it first).

Our 'heroes' and role models were; '*Wilson*' mystery man, consummate athlete, who, clad in his black all-in-one-suit (an early onesie) and equipped with an ancient racquet, won Wimbledon by imparting so much back spin on the ball that his opponent could not reach it before it bounced back on Wilson's side of the net; *Alf Tupper, The Tough of the Track,* trained on a diet of fish and chips and, carrying his spikes and vest in a brown paper parcel, defeated all comers over 800 and 1,500 metres; *Limp along Leslie;* footballer supreme, who by a defect of birth was blessed with one leg shorter than the other which enabled him to curve the ball round any goalkeeper. **I** *flew* **with** *Braddock,* magnificent pilot and leader, refused to Kowtow to any authority, but, wearing the tattered ribbon of his VC, always pulled it off, supported by his faithful navigator 'George'; **Morgan**

The Mighty, a Tarzan figure supported by his faithful servant who wielded the fearsome *Clickiba (*a steel bound cricket bat*)*.

We devoured these stories (and of course the CS Thompson message) play a straight bat, stand up for yourself, never give in to bullies, do the right thing, and the other unfortunate implicit view that 'Johnny Foreigner' was at best a very dodgy cove. The 'Spaniard/Italian' seemed to have a repertoire of underhand tricks to try to beat Alf Tupper on the final bend of the mile race. Not so the black man who always emerged as a 'top chap'. In **Rob Higson's** cricket exploits in the *Rover,* a black, American, ex-service man, called (would you believe) Alabama Cottonfield became an unplayable fast bowler for Highshire CC.

We were quite surprised that picture comics re emerged in the shape of *The Eagle* and *The Lion* and more surprised that we started to read them as well. *The Eagle* was set up to counter the influx of American comics, *Superman, Batman, Spiderman* etc. Its writing personnel were devout Christians, the Rev Marcus Morris of Southport, Chad Varah (Samaritans) and Frank Hampson. The lead story, *'Dan Dare, Pilot of the Future'* was first conceived as *'Lex Christian, the Parson of the Fighting Seventh'* and in the dummy of the first Eagle edition, *'Chaplain Dan Dare'*. Thankfully Hampson decided otherwise, and we happily followed *Dan Dare, Pilot of the Future,* and his sidekick Digby, (who hailed from Wigan and looked like someone who had 'eaten all the pies')*, in his perpetual battle against The Mekon and his Treens.

The Eagle's gimmick was that it was a beautifully illustrated colourful broad sheet and most boys remember it for the exploded diagrams of railway engines, helicopters, liners and space rockets. I can never remember why I bought the *Lion,* which later took over the *Eagle.* You could read it in five minutes. Maybe it was peer pressure or a subtle 'dumbing down' by magazine distributors, who realised that there were more profits to be made catering to the mass market than the upper end.

---

*this is a St Helenian jibe at the expense of Wigan RL supporters and can be seen as graffiti in many places in the town.

The Music Festival (well, the last one)

A long with the annual School Opera, which after *Ruddigore* was never performed again in my lifetime (too many hissy fits in the Green Room perhaps?), there was the School House Music Festival. This was a competitive occasion in which the eight 'Houses' competed in various sections; treble solo, treble choir, tenor/baritone duet, full choir, etc. I was careful to exempt myself from this event as I was still pissed off at 'Chinny' Evers not taking me into the school choir after my brilliant interpretation of 'Jesu lover of my soul'. At the audition, he played a different tune to the one I knew and I sung the thing 'a capella' which I don't think did me any favours. So I watched in the audience as Mike Barrett warbled, 'Where ere you walk', to win the competition; Quel Prat!

The highlight of the festival, which I believe, led to the abolition of the whole shooting match was the Tenor/Baritone duet. In this section it was traditional to have a 'comic song' such as *The Bold Gendarmes* or *A Policeman's Lot* sung by two members of the Sixth Form. But there were new ideas afoot which led to a hilarious rendition of '*I taut I saw a Putty Tat*' by one Prefect (Shanks Davies) in a long black track suit (Sylvester) and the other in a yellow cycle cape (Tweedy Pie). This was topped by a second duo who suitably attired as young swain and well upholstered damsel gave us their version of '*Where are you going to my pretty maid?*' The damsel, who was of course 'going a milking', 'milked' the leg of the grand piano, behind which bottles of milk were concealed. This, naturally, brought the house down. The Cantle was not complementary in his judgement – 'sabotaging the event'... 'bringing the festival into disrepute' – and that was the end of Cowley's imput to the world of music. There were no more festivals of any kind, music or otherwise.

The Work Cup

Last (and least) in this school sketch is the contentious position of the Work Cup. This was a inter house competition designed to assess the quality of the academic work of the school. This after all was the reason that Cowley existed? All the school, with the exception of the Sixth Form were given 'effort' letters at the end of each term. E = Excellent. G = Good. M = Moderate. S= Satisfactory. P = Poor. and U = Unsatisfactory. The scores derived from these individual awards were totalled up to be announced as a House Score at the end of each term. Naturally the winning House got the **Work Cup** at the end of the year. The main letter to avoid was a U, because that would put you 'On Report' and at every lesson you would have to produce a card, which the master would sign to indicate your behaviour and attitude. From Year 1 onwards the volume of applause and enthusiasm tended to diminish in accordance with your seniority and by Year 5 there was a tepid clapping accompanied by low booing when the victor was announced.

When the new Head, (Fred), arrived, he set about tidying up this system, and one of his innovations was to include the Lower Sixth Form in the 'effort letter' scheme. As Sixth Formers we were rather miffed, but having no public examinations in that year, the Boss wanted to keep the pressure on. I cannot remember the full details of what transpired but while we were automatically thinking we, 'The Untouchables', would all get a G grade, *causa honoris*, Joe Draine (History) gave us an M and this required an immediate visit to Fred's study where he gave us the 'hair dryer' treatment, "There must be no slacking off at this point in your school careers. An M does not inspire me with confidence etc, etc." So back we trundled to Joe – "a fine mess you've got us into." Joe was unmoved and while he agreed we were not slacking off, he said that we were working as he would wish us to do at this stage in the term and therefore an M was appropriate. All a question of interpretation. Joe's of course not ours!

Klatu Barada Nikto

The title here is in Martian, which translated means 'Klatu says do not destroy the world.' This was a command given by Klatu (Michael Rennie) to Gort, a ten-foot robot with a laser eye, who had just immolated most of the American armed forces (a slight misunderstanding of course). The film was *The Day the Earth Stood Still*, which still has a place in my 'All Time Schoolboy Greats' alongside *Destination Moon*. At that time we were all still open to novelty. Were there flying saucers out there watching us? Would a manned rocket be able to escape gravity in safety? We were enthralled as the moon spaceship took off and the crew were subject to excruciating G forces, which racked their bodies. ('You wouldn't get me in one of those'). The tension was always heightened by the crew all staring fixedly at 'something out there' with reassuring male hands gripping trembling male shoulders. I was delighted to see, in the latest remake, that Gort was still a giant robot with the laser eye, which so terrified us at the *Rivoli*. But casting John Cleese as the Einstein Prof. was a poor do.

We were all hooked on films. The first Technicolor film I saw of the great western landscape (American west of course) in the plush seats of the St Helens 'Savoy' took my breath away. Colour, space, and scenery you would never imagine. The images portrayed were, of course, totally male dominated. *Shane* is the 'classic' Western. Man rides in to town, man helps honest farmer overcome baddies with impossible gunplay, man rides out again, leaving broken hearted boy and lovelorn farmer's wife. 'Come back Shane' echoes as the *'Faraway Hills'* tune plays. This theme, subsequently reinforced by all Clint Eastwood 'Westerns', and wonderfully lampooned by Mel Brooks' *Blazing Saddles*, was a potent influence on our generation. Men were the doers, the righters of wrongs, courageous and loyal right up to the end (just like their horses). Women were … what? Well definitely not gunfighters. Western women were either faithful wives and mothers (Madonnas), or devious scheming dance hall hussies (Whores). The hero invariably fell for one of the latter but ended up realising what a pinnacle of virtue the girl next door was and married her. But what about those strange women who dressed in leather and carried a riding crop ('I'll tell you when you're older') The cinema has a lot to answer for in our total misunderstanding of woman kind.

We certainly got value for our money in those days as St Helens was replete with cinemas. As the *Reporter* newspaper advertised, '*Don't take you wife for granted, take her to the pictures*'. The 'Savoy' was the best with deep plush carpets, then the 'Rivoli' and the 'Capitol', a bit more spartan. Bang across the road from the '*Riv*' was the 'Hippodrome'. In Oxford Street was the 'Oxford', and last but not least, the 'Scala' (pronounced 'Scayla') were we all saw our first Saturday Matinee (Thrupenny Crush) with *Buck Rogers v Ming the Merciless* and I can say, without contradiction, that the behaviour of the Scala's clientele (us) was appalling. Outlying districts had their own cinemas. Parr naturally had the 'Parvillion'. I can't remember the title of the cinema at Sutton (Empire?*)* but it went by the delightful name of 'The Sutton Bug'. My lasting recollection of the Scala visit was of queuing up outside and being rather bored wondering what would happen if instead of sucking my ice cream through the bottom of the cornet, I blew instead. The ice cream described a gentle arc and landed on the head of some unsuspecting boy further down the line. I just looked the other way.

One of the features of cinema at the time was the 'continuous performance'. The main film and the support film were shown twice from about 5.30 pm so it was common practice for us to go into the cinema at say 6-ish to catch the end of the main picture, then watch the 'B Movie', and then watch all of the main picture again. Reliving the ending of the main film, especially if it was a 'shoot out', and especially as we knew who was going to do what to whom, was a double delight. There was also minimal advertising, just a few slides promoting St Helens retailers, '*Dine in style at the Fleece Hotel*', and then it was on with the show.

I had trouble convincing Dad that we had been in the cinema when I came in at 10.30 pm. 'Were else have you been?' 'Nowhere' 'A fine time to be rolling in'.

The Hippodrome cinema (now a bingo hall) by Ian Grundy

The Capitol cinema (now a fitness suite) by Ian Grundy

It was interesting to observe during our cinema going period, the response to the National Anthem. *God Save the Queen* was played at the end of every show, (as it was at the end of radio and TV transmission) and it was assumed that as the first chord was struck, the audience would stand as a mark of respect. But as time went on this deference diminished. People who did not stand up were 'hissed' at first, but eventually there were only a small remnant of standees while most people walked out. If you were quick you could get into the aisle before the first note was played and then shoot out before everyone else. The live theatres overcame this shambles by playing the Anthem **before** the show to a captive audience.

Big school dinners

L unches, two sittings, were served in a separate building on the 'Top Field'. (This gave us wonderfully long breaks from 12.00 to 2.00.) The hut was long and low, made of rough brick, and not unlike those that cropped up in all prisoner of war camps in films. The masters, on free meals of course, sat in the centre and the diners were ranked on either side. The perk of school dinners for us juniors was getting on the 'fagging' rota for second sitting and serving the sweet course to the assembled masses. You could be a first course fag, serving the main meal, but the best job in the world, was a second course fag, serving the pudding. We would all jostle round the door on Monday to be chosen by the duty master for fagging duties.

Why second course fagging was held in such high esteem was because, after serving all the boys, you were able to go up and get the last dolings out of the sweet, which meant big portions. The last fag in the queue got the biggest sweet, as the cooks scraped every last morsel of Apple Crumble onto your plate. So we fags resorted to various stratagems to make sure that we were last in the queue; hiding in the toilet until the last minute; lying down behind the benches at the far end of the hall and then sprinting up to the hatch to get our reward. (My good luck here was that the Matron, Mrs Prescott, had previously been Head Cook at my former school, Parr Flat Junior, and she was under the illusion that her son, Billy, and I were the best of friends, so I was OK for good meals at all times.) The big laugh was when Kenny Booth left his final dash from his hiding place a little too late and the hatch was closed.

Discipline in the Dining Hall was fairly relaxed but if the noise level became too loud then the Duty Master would shout, 'Stop talking this side/or that side'. Now this command was followed fairly obediently by all, except for the sixth form who were exempt from such trivialities. They just kept on talking.

Now on one occasion Wilf Neilsen, a bear of a boy, and rumoured drug taker, whose whispered command to me was, 'Bring me a large dinner or I'll fuck you,' came into direct confrontation with 'Pam' Morley. Now there was always friction between 'Pam' and the 'Upper School' where he was intensely disliked. On this particular occasion when 'Pam' had issued 'stop talking' orders to both sides of the room, he then issued the unthinkable order, '**sixth form, stop talking**'. You could have heard a pin drop; what would happen next, we were beside ourselves with anticipation. Wilf and his co-diners just pushed back their chairs and still talking simply walked out of the hall.

Sixth form 1, Pam 0.

All you ever think about is sport

Much to my mother's chagrin, sport was now dominating my life especially as I had recently learned that my dad used to play for Everton and Crewe Alexandra. (I wonder if mum had sworn him to secrecy). Disbelievers in the gang were shown the team photo of the Everton 1930 squad, with A. French in the back row alongside such 'immortals' as Ted Sagar, Warny Creswell, and the incomparable 'Dixie' Dean. In the photo, which I still have, 'Dixie' is at the end of the back row on the left. Dad said that he did not turn up for the photo

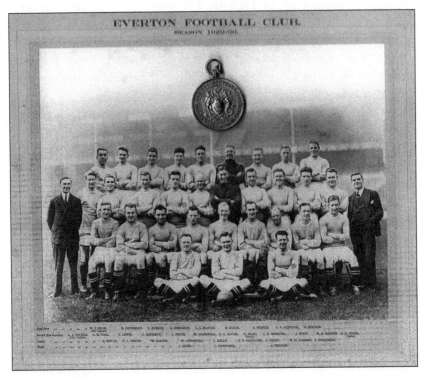

The Everton FC squad 1929/30 with dad's Liverpool Senior Cup winners medal.

and that his picture was pasted in later. Sure enough, if you look obliquely at the photograph you can see the 'stitching' around 'Dixie'. I also learned from dad, and this is a fact that I have never seen published, that 'Dixie' totally hated his nickname and would only answer to 'Billy' (You learned it here first.) Dad also won the Liverpool Senior Cup and gave his medal to his elder brother Joe, which eventually passed into my Trophy Box. I also learned from a contemporary of Dad's, that he had apparently thrown a snooker 'triangle' at 'Dixie' in some dispute. Wow! He could have been famous had he connected.

We 'outlawed' soccer players had found a haven at the YMCA which had a great impact on my life, under its General Secretary, William Walker Leyland. 'Bill' was a 'leader' in every sense of the word. Very skilled in dealing with people, he soon had 'The YM' on the map with a rebuilding programme sponsored by many of the businesses of St Helens. He was the youngest General Secretary ever to qualify in the YMCA and it was no surprise to see him eventually become General Secretary of London YMCA. From that time on I started to 'live' at the YM, even 'popping down' at 9 pm to my father's ire, 'No right thinking person goes out at this hour.' But my defence was now, 'The Epilogue', a very short YMCA evening service, which always took place at 9 pm with tea and biscuits afterwards. Even dad was stumped.

We recruited about four players from our year at Cowley, including the brilliant Arthur Giliker, (think Jimmy Greaves) and romped away with the St Helens 14-16 League and the Harrop Shield beating Holt Sports 6–2. (The only blight on this victory was that I scored a goal but the ref. disallowed it as it had 'gone outside the post' – no goal nets, you see). One of the pluses of playing for the YM was that I could roundly stuff my mates who played for St David's C of E Church team, but who earlier wouldn't let me play for them because I was a 'Baptist'. I think we beat them 9–0 and 16–2. Our league medals were presented to us at a special dinner held at the YMCA by Bill's young wife, the absolutely fabulous Jean (think Penelope Cruz). So more blushes from hot boys. Selection for the St Helens Representative XI convinced me that professional football was just around the corner, as we beat Chester 4–2.

The YMCA team, winners of The Harrop Shield 1954
back row Cunningham, Bellis, Smith, Morgan, Forber
front row French, Giliker, Loftus, Heaton, Sainsbury, Reid

The St Helens JOL (Junior Organisation League) was organised by a nice old chap by the name of Lyndon Phillips, who also umpired in the men's Cricket League. I remember him for his input at meetings when he would say, 'I, *in my wisdom*, have decided etc. etc.' I don't think he was being arrogant it was just his way. The meetings I (as Captain) attended were usually disciplinary ones, when the YM had done something contrary to 'holy writ'.

Two hilarious occasions stand out. The first was the occasion we played Redgate Boys Band on a freezing December afternoon. Some members of both teams turned up early to find a note pinned to the club house door, '*Pitch declared unfit for play due to ice*', signed by the referee. We were undaunted, and, swearing all present to secrecy, their captain threw the note in to the blazing stove. When the rest of our side arrived we said we were 'waiting for the referee' and when he 'failed to appear' we persuaded Arthur Giliker's dad to referee. We won, and poor Mr Giliker, a tad unfit, was laid up in bed for the rest of the weekend. When the truth came out, as it always does, both teams were admonished, but the result stood.

The YMCA team v Redgate with Mr Giliker. An innocent among villains

A more serious crime was the 'Fat' Heaton incident. Brian Heaton was a robust, stockily built centre-forward. He took on his nickname 'Fat' without any worry whatever, but he was always a scrapper. A familiar scene, both teams turn up; no referee; our opponents' secretary says he will referee; game on. 'Fat' turns on his usual performance, smashing in three goals, and felling opponents in his path. At some point, maybe the referee was thinking of saving his boys from further (physical) attack, he sent the rumbustious Heaton from the field of play. 'No way' said Fat, 'You're not a referee anyway, and you're crap' 'Get Off !' 'You get off.' 'Right, I declare this match void.' 'Bollocks', said Fat, 'my dad will ref'. So Mr Heaton refereed the rest of the now void game to the delight of both teams and, of course we were called before the Disciplinary Committee.

'My defence, your honour, was that we i.e. the YMCA team did not agree to the opponents' secretary being the referee.' 'Ah' said Chairman Lyndon, sensing a duel, 'but you must have done, otherwise how did the game take place?' 'He said he would referee', I reposted. 'But you acquiesced, therefore you must have agreed'. My Ciceronian argument that the home team's secretary, as an *adult*, took a unilateral decision to assume the position of referee of a boys' match cut no ice and the game had to be replayed.

Cowley Under 14 Cricket X1 Winners of the Abbot Cup

back row   scorer?, Heath, ??, French R J, Ashton, Fielding, Delaney, Earp, Leigh

Front row   Lawrenson, Litherland, French B, P A Morley, Birkett, Charnock, Beddows.

Seated front Tunstall, McCollum

At school, I was now captain of the U 14s cricket, a member of the St Helens Schools team, and we won the *Abbot Cup*.

Cowley *always* won the *Abbot Cup* defeating all the Sec. Mod. schools in the town. Really it was no contest. We were just bigger and more athletic than the boys of other schools. (In my teaching life I have found this to hold true. All Grammar School sides are taller and bigger than similar age Secondary boys and a hammering is usually on the cards when you play them.) While cricket was the main school sport, athletics also featured in the summer programme. We marvelled at the feats of Ken Friar who could actually clear 5' 8" in the high jump using the western Roll, which I copied assiduously, and 'Flossie' Ingham who could 'catch pigeons' with his school record of 10.4 for the 100 yards. (My dad would have none of this, 'Must be a treacle watch with flannel

School Heroes: Ken Friar clearing 5ft 8in in the High Jump. Still a record today

School Heroes: Shanks Davies, Viking House Captain, leading the tug- of- war team

wheels'). These were our role models and in my scrapbook I still have an autographed picture of Ken Friar in action and the Viking tug-of -war team led by Shanks Davies.

Cowley had what I considered to be a marvellous system for involving us in Athletics participation. Simply put, every boy **had** to enter for a minimum of three events, either two track and one field or two field and one track. The maximum you could enter was five events, split three/two. Entry forms were filled in at House Meetings and the early rounds of competition were completed at lunchtime or after school.

Now of course some of our more un-athletic bretheren would attempt to 'skive off'. But as this was a House competition and you got a point for turning up, there was some pressure to perform. (I am pleased to say that I introduced this scheme in the two Sec. Mods. in which I taught and it worked, even to the point of moving the Sports Day itself to a Saturday (as Cowley's was) to encourage parents to attend, and actually selling the Sports Day programme in the face the opposition of the Head who said I was wasting my time. I could hardly keep a straight face when I told him we'd sold out, but I could let him have my copy.)

My initial choices for the Cowley School Sports were high jump and hurdles (my bankers) then 100 yards, 440 yards and, the event that appealed to the savage in us all, the javelin. It is amazing how young boys pick up a visual picture of an activity and then think they can just do it. As a teacher, I have witnessed in horror a small boy zooming off a trampette and bouncing off the wallbars having attempted his version of a front somersault because he had 'seen his brother do it'. The javelin, as I soon learned, is a very technical event. It is not just chucking a spear. To the howls of laughter from my friends my first attempt, after a stylish run up, hit me on the head and the javelin fell behind me and my second did actually cross the line but was measured (loudly) as 'French, three feet' by some laughing idiot. I forwent my third trial. The 440 yards heats had a similar, though not as comical outcome. Off I went at the gun and by half way I was so far ahead I felt embarrassed. Then lactic acid and the 'stagger' took over and in about fifty yards I went from hero to zero as everybody went past me and I finished last. I never took part in a 440 race again.

My own TV

L ike many families, we got our very own television set, (rented from Granada) for the Queen's Coronation, (gawd bless you ma'am), and didn't it rain that day. The serried ranks of troops splashed up and down the Mall and the massive figure of Queen Salote of Tonga 'won our hearts' by getting soaking wet in her open landau. I can never forget the comment of Noel Coward, when asked by a friend, 'who is the little fellow with Queen Salote?' replied, 'lunch.' The day of the Coronation was also made even more noteworthy, when it was announced that Everest, the unclimable mountain, had at last been conquered by a British team. It must be stated for the record, that the two men who undertook the final ascent were a New Zealander, Edmund Hillary, and a Nepalese sherpa, Tenzin Norgay. But this was a British Expedition, Hillary was British, and the sherpas were topping chaps who had British souls? Or was that the gurkas? Amidst all the hype, I often wondered at the coincidence between the Coronation and the Everest announcement. All a little too pat.

But the arrival of 'the box', soon to be given the name 'idiots' lantern', meant that 'sport', in its myriad forms, could now be viewed day and night. Whether it was Test cricket, where the set was 'warmed up' by dad, so that we could catch the first ball at 11.30 am, or Max Robertson on *Sportsnight* interviewing a very serious Gordon Pirie, who emerged from the fog and rather grumpily disappeared again, after we had heard his heart rate on Max's hand mike, I (plus dad) was there. 'You're in the way', was the joint cry when mum crossed in front of the screen. Thus we (plus mum) cheered to Roger Bannister breaking the 'impossible' four minute mile barrier, Bannister then beating John Landy in the Mile at the Commonwealth Games in Vancouver and Chris Chataway beating the 'unbeatable' Vladimir Kuts under the floodlights at the White City.

We were also witness to the blackest day in English football, or 'The Game of the Century', when England's heroes were annihilated 3–6 by Hungary (the Magical Magyars) on Nov 25 1954. After 13 fog shrouded minutes the score was 1–1 with Sewell equalising Hideguti's opener. We sat back and waited for the customary England victory. But at half time we were 1–4 down and 3–6 at the close, with Ferenc Puskas leaving my personal favourite Billy Wright on his backside with a fantastic dummy and blasting the ball past poor Gil Merrick. This ignominy was repeated with interest six months later in the Nep Stadion when Hungary won 7–1. Fortunately it was not televised direct. More than anything these defeats signalled to the press our continuing decline as a major player on the world stage'.

Once TV became part of the furniture, we watched as much as we could ie anything that was on besides sport, from *Café Continental, 'Bonjour Madames, Messieurs'* to the *Grove Family;* from *'Tonight'* (with Cliff Michelmore) to *Dixon of Dock Green (Evenin' all)*. We were all suitably terrified by *'The Quatermass Experiment'* of 1953 when poor old Victor Caroon was shot into space and came back as a cactus. (How daft could you get?) Dafter it would seem, as *'Quatermass II'* followed in 1955 with meteorites, containing embryonic aliens, landing in England and being put into giant vats to be hatched out, and of course take over the world. Brian Donlevy, as Prof Quatermass, was magnificent as he bumbled about in what looked like a cardboard overcoat. *'Quatermass and the Pit'* in 1958 was my favourite and I still have my

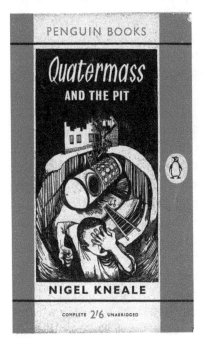

The original Penguin script of 'Quatermass and The Pit'... very scary.

69

Penguin copy of the original screenplay, but the plot is too complicated to relate, (we were all supposed to be Martians), but I still have memories of Colonel Breen, (Anthony Bushell) burnt to a crisp. (He should have listened to the Prof).

ITV brought adverts to our screen in 1955, which were much more entertaining than their programmes. Who cannot be moved to recall those early hymns of praise; 'the Esso Sign', 'Armour Star' or 'Rael Brooke Toplin', which for younger readers was a dancing shirt which didn't need ironing. Of course it was a matter of class, pride and snobbery that 'one' did not 'really' watch ITV. 'One' really preferred the BBC; Ohh ... Richard Dimbleby, Ohh ... The Brains Trust, Ohh ... Sir Mortimer Wheeler – sooo sophisticated. And of course they were. ITV decided to pitch for 'the people's market' following the American influence; game shows and Soaps which proved universally successful. What market today's Sky TV is targeting is best left unsaid (and unwatched).

Boxing in the 1950's was very much a socially acceptable sport. We had all done some boxing at junior school, on 'wet' games days and most families possessed a pair of boxing gloves in order to teach their sons 'how to look after themselves'. At Mickey Daybell's birthday parties, 'boxing' was the highlight of the evening and we gleefully pummelled each other into submission in the 'ring' made by the chairs of their parlour suite. If there was a 'big fight' on the radio I 'stayed up' with dad. We were happy listeners when Randolph Turpin achieved the impossible, taking the World Middleweight Championship from Sugar Ray Robinson on 10 July 1951 at Earls Court only to loose it in the return fight in September in New York.

(When one considers that there was only two months separating these murderous bouts, it says something for the fitness of the fighters, if not the avariciousness of their managers.)

We were even more delighted when the jungle drums announced that Eric Marsden, a successful flyweight, and St Helens boy, was actually coming to live just round the corner in Chadwick Road. Eric was due to fight the Welsh champion Dai Dower for the British Flyweight title in August 1955. A

'Marsden Watch' was set up and his movements were recorded. Saw EM running; saw EM going for paper; saw EM in front garden etc. In the flesh he was a very mild looking chap and very pleasant to all. Unfortunately he just could not make the big time. He only lost three fights but they were crucial ones and Dai Dower easily out pointed him over 15 rounds. The sound of W. Barrington – Dalby's inter-round summaries filled us with gloom, 'Well', he drawled, 'that was again Dower's round'. There could only be one result.

I think we realised the real trauma of boxing when poor old Don Cockell (British Champion) was put up for the World Heavyweight Championship title against 'Rocky' Marciano, on 16 May 1955 in San Francisco. Marciano was a compact slugger who just kept coming forward and however hard he was hit, hit back even harder and more often. Cockell had had enough by Round nine. Marciano, who retired undefeated, won by Technical Knock Out. Fighting the Americans was suicide as Bruce Woodcock found out when he was hammered (broken jaw) by another US slugger Joe Baksi. (The idea of a Brit becoming a World Champion was a pipe dream).

A rare photograph of the boxer Eric Marsden

Modes of transport ▪ ▪ ▪ ▪ ▪

lmost without exception we travelled to school by bus or
walked. Both of these activities were unaccompanied by
any responsible adult. No 'responsible' adult would ever
think of taking a child to school. Conversely, no child would
be seen dead in the presence of an accompanying parent. Getting
to school on the bus was however a bit of a bind. To get the
solitary direct bus which passed Cowley School we had to leave
home at 7.30 am and do a brisk half mile run/walk with various
items of kit, to be sure of getting the '8.10 am Circular'. This
dropped us at school at 8.30, giving us a freezing half hour to kick
around before we were let into school. The two-bus route, into
town and out, had its advantages. You did not need to get out
as early, or have to walk as far, just down the street, for the No
55, and the second bus to Denton's Green (No 8 Trolley bus) was
full of those strange, entrancing sirens, 'Cowley Girls' in their
green uniforms. The drawbacks were that if 'The 55' was full you
were stuffed. In our usual dilatory state, we often ran the gauntlet
of arriving just in time to miss the 8.10 Circular, and then having
to run all the way back uphill to try to catch the 55.

Travelling by St Helens Corporation Transport in those days
would today be classed as a health risk or an abuse of minors.
We all wanted to ride 'upstairs' on the 'Double Deckers' especially
at the front. If we were allowed 'on top' by the conductor, who
more often than not would make us go 'inside', we then we able
to rebreathe the smoke from the cigarettes of thirty odd men
on their way to work. At the front of the top deck of all buses
was the admonition, *'Spitting Prohibited'* (a friend of mine
visiting from Harrow just could not believe it. But we did have
some standards).

We also discovered that those same stairs were most revealing
of the legwear of 'St Helens finest' as they tottered down them in
their wide skirts and starched petticoats. So sitting downstairs at

the back also had its own advantages for grubby boys. Nearly all buses then had open rear entrances, which made it quite easy to jump on and off when the bus was in motion (in St Helens speak this was known as 'cogging on' or 'off'.) We soon mastered the technique which was especially useful when the bus slowed down to take a corner provided of course that you remembered to jump off in the same direction as the bus was travelling, if not you were flat on your back – to the hilarity of all onlookers. The danger of the open platform was emphasised when Bill Dixon's mum completely forgot where she was and calmly walked off the bus, as it was still moving. Luckily she survived this accident. Even my dad had a cautionary tale of attempting to board a moving trolley bus at the Town Hall. He slipped off the platform, but holding on to the rail was dragged across the square. 'Well that's the end of that suit', as they say in the movies.

Car ownership was beyond my family's expectations as it was for most families in the post war period. My uncle Arthur who was a bit 'flash' (member of the Masons etc) had a *Hillman Shooting Brake* (whatever that was) and that was it. The cynosure of all eyes in our street, Litherland Crescent, was the black *Triumph Mayflower* of Mr Tom Brown, which stood immaculate on his driveway. In the years before 'St Helens Corpy' got round to tarmacing the side roads, Litherland Crescent was a potholed dirt track (ideal for any game you could think of). When 'The Browns' were going to town, we would watch as Mr Brown very, very slowly drove his pride and joy over the potholes and down to the main road and the Brown Family (Mrs B, Jack, Barbara and Dorothy) walked alongside the car as if they were accompanying a hearse. It was quite a performance.

From year two onward we were allowed to come to school on our bikes. Halleluja! My dad, who had refused to buy me a bike for passing 'The Scholarship', ('You would be lethal on a bike') had succumbed to my constant pressure and I was not to be denied, especially after he said he **had** got me a bike and then gave me drawing of one. (Can you believe such cruelty?) It just made me all the more determined. However my vision of a drop handlebar racer with ultra thin tyres was not to be. It was a new Raleigh or nowt. This was a heavy brute with sit up and beg handlebars, a crank case and an integral dynamo. No one in his right mind would ride this pansy affair. So my sympathetic friends set to work with a will. Spanners in hand, we first took out the handlebars and turned them over giving them a quarter drop position, like my mate Brian Wilson's, then we just had to get rid of that crank case. I mean what was the use of having a bike if you couldn't get oil on your trousers. The dynamo 'just didn't work' – not after we'd finished with it anyway. So equipped with an acceptable machine I was ready to cycle to school with the 'gang'.

The sit up and beg Raleigh. The all steel beast.

Cowley School is at the top of Hard Lane, one of the steepest hills in St Helens. If your bike had multiple Derailleur gears you could ride up it, but it was not a mark of disgrace to get off and walk, which most of us did, only having the Sturmey Archer three speed. Coming home was a different story. Speed of descent was of the essence and if you could get enough speed up down the hill you could free wheel for almost another mile, if of course you could negotiate (i.e. ignore) the left hand turn into the main road at the bottom of the hill, past Hatton's Garage, and the right turn across the traffic into Washway Lane. The competition to see who could free wheel the furthest was intense. For me it came to an abrupt end when, with me hammering homeward down the hill, a small boy decided that it would be a good idea to run across the road to his mum. I remember sailing over the handlebars and crashing down on the tarmac, trousers ripped and beloved bike twisted out of shape. Then the natural sympathy of St Helens folk for 'the fallen' came to the surface. No one gave a toss about me, all they could think about was this idiot boy and his mum. At last as I was walking off with my bruises, a woman said, 'They should have given you the cup of tea love, not him, it wasn't your fault.' I walked on home, in the gathering dark, pushing my wreck. The strong are lonely.

Bikes gave you access to fields afar, well not that afar. One of our 'big ideas' was to ride to Southport, something that my Dad and cousin John had done in their youth, or claimed they had. With a following wind and a pack of sandwiches we just about made it to the outskirts of Ormskirk before giving up. Our regular trips were biking to Dovecote Baths, always cold, and down the East Lancs Road to Golborne for train spotting. Golborne was on the Euston – Glasgow line and the express trains pulled by Coronation Class engines were magnificent to behold as they thundered past our perch on the bank beside the track. With our basic box cameras we could get good photos of them if we could catch them coming head on. This sometimes entailed lying down as close as possible to the track to get the shot. On one notable occasion Eddie Duncan and myself decided to cycle to Golborne, despite the fact that it was forecast to be unsettled. Sure enough the rain came sweeping across the tracks and we decided to call it a day. Now Eddie had a 'fixed wheel' bike, which could work up a good head of steam, but the bike had no mud guards. My memory of the return ride home is of being behind Eddie all the way and watching this ever thickening line of mud spreading from his backside up to his head. Freezing but funny.

The joys of railway photography These small pics were the biggest we could shoot.

Trainspotting took up a fair amount of our time and we were often prowling the platforms of Wigan North Western station with our Ian Allen LMS books and cheese sandwiches. I can remember putting the fear of God into one unfortunate who threw his orange peel onto the track. I casually observed that he might just have derailed the 'Mid Day Scot', which was due next. It was one of those frightening moments in childhood when you know logically something cannot be true i.e. a massive locomotive would not be derailed by an orange peel but you can't really accept it. The wheels could skid .... I think we were both quite relieved when the train had passed. Of course competition was keen to see who had clocked the most namers' (trains with nameplates on them). Elusive engines like *'The Artists Rifleman'* *'The Duchess of Abercorn'*, *'The Patriot'*, were sought in vain. Sometimes we whooped with delight as *'The Clan McLeod'* or the new *'Britannia'* (with external Caprotti valve gear) thundered past. Back home the 'spotted' trains were carefully underlined in red. It was a fortunate boy indeed who was able to purchase the Ian Allen *Combined Edition* all the four regions' trains, with photos, in one volume. They cost the then unaffordable price of £5 (and of course Brian Wilson had one.)

Our train spotting mania was a trifle weird. One year we were at the School Summer camp in Abergele and, as tradition had it, one day of the week was set aside for us chose our own activity. So 'Fags' Fielding (who needlessly ran me out against Prescot Grammar and smoked a pipe) suggested to me, 'Willie' (B. Wilson) and 'Spudder' (Woods), that we should go to Chester Station for the day. Expedition approved by PAM, off we went. The search for Southern Region 'namers' was proving futile by lunchtime, so what more natural that we should hop aboard a southbound train for Crewe; 'Mecca' for all spotters and replete with 'sheds' into which we hoped we might sneak. A good time was had by all until we decided that someone should look up the train times back to Chester and thence Abergele. We found to our dismay that we would probably get back to camp round about 9 pm after a walk from Abergele station in the pitch black dark. Now as PAM had slippered a whole gang of us that morning just for talking in the huts before 7.30 am, what dire punishment would he mete out to us defaulters. We swore that no one would confess to the Crewe expedition but we would stick to the story of 'delays at Chester'. 'Sorry Sir just our bad luck'. PAM just used his favourite expression, 'You half wits', turned on his heel and disappeared. I don't know who was the more relieved.

Abergele Camp from where we planned our great trainspotting adventure.

'Music, music, music' (and other distractions)

Music has always featured strongly in my life. My mother's (Welsh) family were musical, grandfather was a tenor, and my grandmother, and aunt all played piano and organ properly i.e. with the pedals. My mother was a good pianist. My father had a fine baritone voice and always sang snatches of Peter Dawson round the house, *The Diver, Boots, The Gay Highway*. He and his three brothers could play the mandolin. My uncle, Bill, who also made one string fiddles, later taught me the mandolin but not until I had escaped from the drudgery of learning to play the piano which I was embarked on at the age of seven. How I hated 'practice', especially when football was a much more attractive option. I had a very good 'ear' for a tune and so I used to play any piece, once I had learned it, by ear, and hadn't a clue where I was on the actual page. My 'Eleven Plus pass' was the ticket to escape from the keyboard. I argued successfully that I would have too much homework to carry on playing. I never did find out why my mother accepted this flimsy excuse. Maybe even she had pity for the suffering. I had no regrets despite dire warnings from all and sundry that I would be sorry later on.

At school we were all aficionados of the new *Hit Parade*, first published in *New Musical Express* on 14 Nov 1952, tuning in to the *Saturday Club* and Radio Luxemburg ('208 on your dial'), and like all children we learned the words of all the songs effortlessly; Guy Mitchell, *She Wears Red Feathers*; Frankie Laine, *Champion the Wonder Horse*, Alma Cogan, *Bell Bottom Blues* (I can still bore the pants off any audience with my rendition of *Does you Chewing Gum lose its flavour on the bedpost overnight?*). As the decade progressed, we watched the *Six Five Special* and *Juke Box Jury* with the urbane chairman David Jacobs. I grew particularly fond of panellist Jack Payne, the grumpy old bandleader, who seemed to loathe all pop music, giving most records 'A Miss'. Then of course 'the Guitar' suddenly appeared with Bill Haley and his Comets. Theatres were wrecked; the devil was loose in St Helens! We crowded into the Rivoli Cinema to see if Elvis Presley would cause us all to go crazy. No, *'Love Me Tender'* was OK but nowt special.

Of course we were now members of that new, strange group, 'Teenagers' who, almost as part of their contract, sneered at almost everything, sulked (until they got a boy/girlfriend), totally hated their parents, and had galloping acne. It is a well-known fact that any adolescent child having a pimple on their chin, knowing that it will subside in its own good time, will squeeze it – especially if they are 'going out'. I was seduced by something called *Teen Creem*, a concoction to 'banish teenage spots'. This lotion was to be spread liberally over the face, then you were to place said face over hot steaming water, and watch all the poisons squirting out of your acnied pores. Of course what was wriggling out of your pores was the cream you had liberally slapped on. It was quite spectacular and kept me occupied in front of the bathroom mirror until acne just disappeared unprompted.

Nearly everybody I knew either had a guitar or knew someone who had one. I was fortunate that one of my mates, Bill Dixon, not only had a guitar, but his Dad, who was a pattern maker at Forster's glassworks, could actually MAKE them. Bill's dad could make anything. In the hall of their house was a magnificent rendition of *The Laughing* Cavalier in fretwork and on the mantle piece were birds carved out of ivory. Many of the lads who bought guitars in the initial frenzy, couldn't play them, so I, who was by now monopolising Bill's guitar, picked up a 'cello guitar' for £70 from a Cowley boy, whose name I have forgotten, but who I think 'went out' with my cousin Marie. From then on, Bill and I warbled our way through Lonnie Donnegan's entire oeuvre until either Mrs Dixon threw us out or my dad came to collect me – *(Ol' Reilly don' gone like a turkey through the corn yeh, Hey Rattler Hey)* And Bill and his dad built a guitar with the deepest sound box ever made. I wonder what happened to it?

One of the great debates, which raged in our school gang was

Traditional v Modern Jazz. Our introduction via Mr Donnegan was to 'Chris Barber and his Traditional Jazz Band' (Lonnie played banjo) but soon we were really 'moved' by the sound of Muggsy Spanier and *At the Jazz Band Ball*. It became very difficult to explain to any 'sensible adult' exactly why this music had such an effect. But as we knew, we were a different generation. Dig! The Theatre Royal held several Jazz concerts, which were packed out. My chief recollection of which is an Alex Welch concert when I put my knees up on the back of the seat in front and got the most painful cramp in my thighs. I staggered up the aisle and the poor usherette must have thought I was drunk. 'Cramp, cramp', I said lying down flat at the top of the stairs. The rift came when Brian Wilson, who took the New Musical Express, the mark of a true believer, announced that 'trad jazz' was too predictable and 'modern jazz' was what the intellectual should be listening to. Now I could go along with some of Stan Kenton and Ted Heath, but Jacques Lousier and his Trio with their little beards, no thanks.

Another of our musical icons was the American mathematician Tom Leherer. Leherer was a satirist of the first order, a droll comedian and an excellent pianist. His first recording, *The Elements*, a list of the periodic table of the elements set to Gilbert and Sullivan's *Major General Song*, was a gentle introduction to his lyrical attacks on nearly all of America's sacred cows; university, scouts, army, 'my home town', after which he just let rip at anything with *The Masochism Tango*, *The Old Dope Peddle'* and *Poisoning Pigeons in the Park* (*… and maybe we'll do in a squirrel or two.*) 'Songs by Tom Leherer' was the first Long Playing (33.3 revs per min) record I ever bought, even though I did not have a record player, but in such satire we were witnessing the first rumblings of discontent with a pre WWII status quo which our parents had sought to resurrect. And so the pot began to simmer with protest singers, Bob Dylan and Joan Baez leading to the civil rights movement and Martin Luther King. The times were a changin'.

Working class pastimes

Despite Cowley's hopes of higher pursuits for its alumnae, we clung to our working class pastimes. Fishing (coarse) was one of them. Picture the cream of St Helens youth, sheltering from the rain under a coal wagon while casting their lines out into the swirling waters of the St Helens Canal, or 'The Hotties' as the place was known. This was where the hot overflow from Pilkington Glassworks flowed into the canal. (It was also

'The Hotties' then and now.

where everybody put their unwanted goldfish). Bill Dixon and Bob Marsh were proper fisherman. I sort of tagged along, agreeing to a 6.30 am start for Carr Mill Dam, knowing full well that I would get down to the waterside at about 10.o'clock, being overjoyed to find out that they 'hadn't had a tickle all morning'. Bill had the angling works; keep nets, disgorger, stool, fixed spool reel, catapult for shooting ground bait out into the best areas. I had my Uncle Hughie's old three-piece trout rod, which had the disconcerting habit of coming apart at some time in the day and floating off down stream. Its eventual demise (I couldn't be bothered to wade in again to get it) led me to the purchase of *'The Edgar Sealy Octofloat Deluxe Rod'* from Booth's Sports Shop in Hardshaw Street, for the incredible sum of five pounds. This was a five piece, split cane, state of the art rod and at least put me on a par with my fishy compatriots. My two outstanding 'catches' were a jack pike (small) at Walton Reservoir, and a 15 ounce roach at Carr Mill, which I carried home on the rod, hoping to impress the people in the bus queue at Derwent Road. Mum actually cooked it after washing it out with about a ton of salt to get rid of the rather 'earthy' taste.

Living as we did on the edge of town with the countryside at hand we followed country practices. Everybody, without exception, swam in The Dam in summer, and went home bright red with sunburn. Carr Mill Dam was a huge expanse of water which served as a feeder to the Sankey Canal via 'the Steps', an algae coated outflow of 30 steps on which many an unwary reveller slipped. The great fear was of being washed all the way down 'The Steps' until you finally bobbed up in the quieter waters of Happy Valley. Many a good tale was told of this experience – all lies of course. The railway viaduct over Happy Valley was a proving ground for the most daring. I remember witnessing Albert Taylor crossing it hand over hand on the underside of the girders. (He also walked waist deep in the liquified 'burgy' when we all fully expected him to disappear for good. (Now he was mad!)

The one feature of Carr Mill Dam and the surrounding countryside was that it was virtually impossible to develop or

The Nineteen Arches on Carr Mill Dam by Robbob

A dream of Carr Mill Dam – a painting by the author from a line
drawing

police. Over the years, several business companies tried. Walls were built, barbed wire fences were erected and turnstiles put in place, supposedly to bring in revenue. A sort of early safari park idea. All to no avail. It was all too easy to find a way in. The only feature that grew in popularity was Hydroplane Racing on summer's weekend. The noise was tremendous and echoed over the whole district to the anger of the more sedate residents. (It was the equivalent of living next door to a motor strimmer fanatic). The hydroplanes were here to stay and still zoom up and down the Dam to this day.

The noisy neighbours – Speedboats on the Dam by Robbob

Collectables

█ █ █ █ █

Everyone kept birds eggs, the rule being that if you found a nest you could only take one egg out of it. ('Rogging' i.e. taking all the eggs was a heinous crime.) Dad was amazing at spotting nests. I would be staring blankly at some hedge or other and he would just put his hand into the foliage and out would come an egg. Mum, who usually was the epitome of femininity, would 'blow' the egg, making two holes at either end and gently blowing the yolk out. So I finished up with quite a good collection, augmented I should add by some specimens like a cormorant's egg that Dad got from 'a chap down Parr' (sink of urban depravity!).

Other 'collectibles' were stamps; we sold and swapped these at school. Tanou Tuva 'triangulars', owned (of course) by my best friend Brian Wilson, were much coveted. Stamp companies had a great business going. Every person who ordered *'Approvals'* was given a free packet of assorted stamps. Most of us were hawking our books of stamps around the school, collecting the money and sending a cheque off in the Post. (Possibly our first introduction to the world of business.)

Later in the senior school the prize *entrepreneur* was 'Butch' Wilson. 'Butch' sold Football Fixed Odds sheets for a local bookie but his 'cheek' was to get the package sent to school for him to collect from the school office. It was amusing to get a lesson interrupted by a messenger from the school office requesting that Mr Wilson should pick up a package at break. Butch's reign as *Mr Big* came to a sad end when, like all failed businessmen, he decided to 'stand some bets' i.e. taking the stake money and not laying any bets. Someone laid into him and his bookmaking career came to an end.

Cigarette packets were also favoured items. Such exotics as *'Passing Cloud'*, *'Markovitch Black and White'*, and *'State Express 333's'* graced my Ciggy Album along with the standards,

Capstan Full Strength, Navy Cut, Craven A ('Does not affect your throat', said both footballer Stanley Matthews and racing driver Stirling Moss) and *Strand* (with which 'you were never alone'). As a cigarette, the *Strand* 'bombed' on the market. The vast smoking public did not wish to be associated with the Lonely Man who had no friends. No one had yet tied together smoking and lung cancer, in fact no one dared speak the disease's name (your granddad died of 'C'.) At that time 79% of men were smoking on average 15 per day. Our smoking exploits were very tame. Rolled up bits of newspaper sufficed but the St Helens and District Reporter never made a good smoke and it didn't light fires either. I can't recall ever smoking a proper cigarette before I went to University in 1959.)

The traditional laminated pre war cigarette cards were no longer available with the cigarettes but there was a substitute. The back of each packet of 10 *'Turf'* Cigarettes had a picture in a series, aircraft, animals etc. Not many people smoked *'Turf'* (they were said to taste like turf or worse) so we avid collectors had to trawl building sites, and always keep an eye on the gutter of the street in case a rare gem was lying there. Even wet packets were lovingly dried out. I actually achieved the full count of 52 aircraft. 'YR Sauce' brought out a series of badges of Football Teams (one badge per bottle). If you used enough sauce to collect all the badges you would win a real leather football. Soused in sauce, Brian Wilson sent in his badge collection for the prize, which was something of a disaster; an out of shape, thin leather object of derision. What a hoot!

Our obsession with all things sporting introduced us to the most wonderful time waster/wet weather passer/idle moment filler, and that was **'OWZAT'**, a very simple cricket game played with two small, hexagonal steel bars. One bar had the figures 1,2,3,4,6, 'Owzat' on its faces and the second bar had methods of being given out i.e. Bowled, LBW, Caught, Stumped, Run Out, and Not Out. So the 'batsman' rolled the numbered bar and if it rested on 'Owzat' the 'fielder' rolled the 'umpires bar' for the decision. (Poorer members of our community made do with two bits of hexagonal HB pencil on which they wrote the legends).

We used real scoring books, purchased from Benny Brookes Sports and had teams; Lancs v Yorks; England v Australia; Footballers v Cricketers; even Comedians v Glamour Girls. (Diana Dors once made 140 not out against the bowling of Groucho Marx.)

It was 'Subbuteo' however, the table football game, devised by P. A. Adolph, that took up much of our leisure – and our pocket money. These small cardboard figures standing in their hemispheric plastic bases were able to be flicked at the small facsimile ball to score goals in the small goal nets. You could make the players pass to each other and swerve round opponents. And you could buy a green baize pitch with all the markings. So from small cardboard beginnings, Blue (Everton) v Red (Liverpool), Mr Adolph, with our help, built his business. Soon we could buy plastic players in all English and Scottish strips and referees and floodlights. I remember the joy of getting 'Tottenham' and 'Arsenal' in the post. There were international competitions and a 'Subbuteo' magazine. (Eventually the players became 3D, moulded on the human figure, but by then we had 'moved on'.) My dad, who thought Subbuteo was a monumental waste of time and money, 'killed' Tommy Eglington the Everton Number 11, when he sat on him in one of games played on the parlour (front room) floor. (I was quite relieved to find that B. Wilson (best mate) had invested his cash in *Newfooty*, a far inferior product. The bases of the players were so hard you nearly broke your flicking finger.)

(The name Subbuteo has its own history. Adolph wanted to call his new game Hobby, but the games manufacturers protested that he was trying to take their business. So the enterprising P.A. chose this strange name Subbuteo which is Latin for the bird of prey, 'Hobby'.)

'Having a gun' also became something of a must (or in my case a mustn't). Guns of all kinds were part of our childhood culture. Pop guns, Cap guns, Potato Pistols, Elastic guns – you name it, we had it. The US 'Western' influence was paramount. Brian Wilson had relatives in the States, who sent him a large, silver six shooter with a revolving chamber. Green with envy, we all wanted to handle this treasure, but he was unmoved to our pleadings, quite enjoying his gun-owning superiority. We would have killed to have a relative in America, anybody, second cousin twice removed. All of which was forgotten when real guns came on the scene.

For many parents real guns were anathema. Everyone knew someone whose child had lost an eye in a pellet gun accident. Despite my assurances that my responsibility was unimpeachable, the answer was **NO.** So just like the TV 'quest', you had to find someone who had a piece of armament. Now some boys had air rifles, Maurice and Geoff Leyland had a *Webley* Air Pistol with which we used to shoot wasps with match sticks as ammo, Bill Dixon had a spring loaded *Gat,* and Nev Greenall paraded round with a genuine double barrelled shotgun! ('Go on Nev giz a hold'). Tom Monoly, a hulking, armed, seventeen-year-old, lined us all up against Stratton's shop wall and made Tubby Tinsley 'kiss the ground'. I surreptitiously 'borrowed' Bill Dixon's *Gat.* This was a magnificently underpowered piece of ordnance. You could actually see the flight of 'the slug' as it winged (crawled) its way to its target. I once shot a crow from ten feet and it just looked at me in disdain. My other successes were decapitating a tulip in the garden by accident, and bagging a very unlucky sparrow, sitting on our chimney pot, which actually swallowed the bullet. I never returned the *Gat* to Bill and somewhere on life's journey it just disappeared.

One other figure in our 'country life' should be mentioned and that was Cowleian Barry Halpin. He was older than us but was into all sorts of country pursuits and he played a mean accordion. But he was a loner, an emerging eccentric. Moving on several decades I was surprised, along with many Cowleians, to see Barry's unmistakable features staring at us from the pages of the press under the banner, *'Lord Lucan found in Puket'.* Some (now rather disappointed) author had come to the conclusion that a bohemian character called 'Jungly Barry', who lived in some exotic paradise, was none other than the murderous Lord Lucan. 'It's only Barry Halpin' said *le tout* St Helens. We don't fool easily.

Real politics

L ike all aspiring schools Cowley was proud of its Debating
Society and put on events like 'balloon debates' and lectures
by staff and students. Ray French astounded us all with his
illustrated lecture on the Mayan Civilisation. I was 'elected' as
Secretary i.e. no one else wanted to write up the proceedings and
so I got lumbered. However the big event in 1956, our GCE Year,
was the Suez Crisis and a debate was put on the agenda with the
(rather portentous) title, *This House deplores the action of Her
Majesty's Government in their illegal action against Egypt'*.
I chose to speak against the motion. In the first place, I was usually
against anything that everyone else was for, my argumentative
nature being best inscribed in the staff comment on my report,
'Me thinks he doth protest too much.' But I could not see anything
illegal in the action of Britain and France in protecting national
and international trade by keeping The Canal open. France had
built the thing and we had financed it, so Nasser's decision to
nationalise it seemed to me at the time as just piratical. I made the
simple point that Nasser had promised to keep his hands off The
Canal in return for our withdrawal of troops from the Canal
Zone, and he was in breach of the 1888 Agreement re the
management of the canal (So much for trusting yer Arab). The
upshot was that I and my fellow speaker defeated the motion.

For us, The Suez Crisis was remembered with affection, for a
completely different reason. Petrol rationing was in force and
as an addition The Driving Test was suspended for one year,
which meant that learners could drive unaccompanied. Now Bill
Dixon was learning to drive, and his dad had a Standard Eight.
So our fishing trips now became motorised, as with Bill at the
wheel we explored further flung waters. I vividly recall such a day
at Leigh Flash. It was drizzling and a small stream was running
down into the main body of water. Just at that point we hit a shoal
of perch obviously feeding on whatever was being brought down

on the stream. It was fishy heaven. Maggot; cast; strike; perch; disgorger; keep net. It made up for all those barren days, watching your bobbing float and 'drowning bread' (dad's joke). Sometimes in bed, I could still see the float and the lapping water as I tried to go to sleep.

In December of that year, however, we were witness to the consequences of 'real politics'. We were invited to a meal at the St Helens YMCA to meet a party of Hungarian refugees who had fled the country in the wake of the brutal suppression of 'the Uprising' by the Russian army. From their appearance the men had escaped in the clothes they stood up in. But they were alive, and thankful. It did not go unnoticed that Russia could point to our earlier intervention in Suez as a justification of her attack on Hungary. My debating victory seemed a little hollow.

There was no doubt that 'Suez' was a national turning point. Depending on your viewpoint we either lost our credibility as a 'moral' nation, or we lost our bottle as a 'decisive' nation. I am inclined to the latter view. As a result of our dithering over Suez, petrol prices rocketed and our 'desertion' of France made sure that De Gaulle would say 'non, non, et non' to our entry into Europe. Of course, viewing Suez in hindsight the whole affair was a political nightmare with so many cooks stirring so many pots with so many conflicting recipes that a 'fiasco' was inevitable.

Another matter which exercised us somewhat was the 'strong possibility' (according to the Press) that all our puny efforts would evaporate (literally) when the world self combusted in the Nuclear Chain Reaction which would be set off when our scientists released 'The H Bomb', or when the West and the East began their policy of **Mutually Assured Destruction.**

As Tom Lehrer put it:-

If the bomb that drops on you
Gets your friends and neighbours too
There'll be no body left behind to grieve
And ... we ... will ...
All go together when we go
All suffused with an incandescent glow

So just sing your last 'Te Deum'
When you see that ICBM
We will all go together when we go

Our fears were not without some support. It appeared that the only way to be acknowledged as a 'World Power' was to develop a series of super bombs with ever more apocalyptic explosions. These were measured, in the Press, in how many times they were more *'powerful than Hiroshima*. The 'Our bomb is better then Your bomb contest' was carried out throughout the Fifties. In October of 1952 we exploded our very own Atom Bomb off the Montebello Isles in Australia. The US upped the ante by detonating a Hydrogen Bomb at the Eniwetock Atoll in the Pacific (that should be the ex Eniwetock Atoll). In August 1953 the Russians banged off a hydrogen bomb and the US replied with a bigger hydrogen blast at the Bikini Atoll in 1954. The Russians went two better with hydrogen explosions in 1955 and 1957. And so it went on until (thankfully) the Russians, who actually were rubbish at making bombs, started a new game of 'Our Satellite is better than Your Satellite' – and we'll be in space afore ye', with the launch of *Sputnik 1* on 4 October 1957 and, just to ram home the point, with *Sputnik 2* in November with a live dog, *Laika*, on board. Politics aside, we were enthralled with *Sputnik* pinging out its 'beep beep' call sign over the airwaves and even more excited when the Russians actually managed to reach the moon with *Luna 2* in 1959. When their (and our) smiling hero Yuri Gagarin stepped down in triumph from *Vostok 1* after successfully orbiting the earth in 108 minutes, the Russian triumph was complete and launched the next contest, 'We can do more orbits of the earth than you can'. It was left to the Kennedy administration to come up with the 'big one'; putting a man on the moon and bringing him back. A magnificent macho coup; inordinately expensive and as De Groot (2011) argues 'a virility symbol without much real development when compared with satellite technology.

Have you done your homework?

The big difference between ourselves and our Sec. Mod. mates was that while they had 'sort of' homework' that they 'sort of' did' or not, we **did** have it and it **had** to be done. What was the point of going to Cowley if you couldn't complain about homework? On the rare occasions where Mr X hadn't given us any, our parents didn't believe us anyway. The schedule was three subjects per night ranging from 40 minutes each in year one to infinity as we got older. Like piano practice it wasn't football, but we just settled down to working every night after tea 'till almost bed time with such delights as 'A Time Line of Hamurappi's Empire'; 'Irregular French verbs which take etre'; 'The use of the Ablative Absolute'. (*Yes*, we could have started homework as soon as we came in from school and, *yes*, we could have had it finished before tea, but as we were not characters in some Enid Blyton story; we just didn't). The game was to see how long it was into the evening before someone noticed that you were 'really interested' in Panorama on TV and kicked you upstairs. Some homework seemed to expand to fill up any gap in time, Latin being a case in point. 'Kipper' Addshead dominated our weeks with translations from the 'set books', *The Aeneid* or *The Georgics*. 'Just prepare 500 lines for tomorrow'. Come the morrow and our 500 lines construed, he would then say something like, 'Yes not bad, now keep up the flow and we'll carry on with the next 500 tomorrow'. No wonder no one ever failed Latin, it seemed to be all that we did.

Weekends were wonderful; two days to put time (and homework) on hold. So, you couldn't do any homework on Friday night (Youth Club) and you had Saturday and Sunday to do it. On Saturday morning you could get up just late enough to be rushing to get your kit ready for whatever afternoon game you were playing, and you always had to meet at the YM well in advance. Saturday night – you must be joking. So that left Sunday. Now my favourite time to do homework was Sunday morning. If I started then I would know how much time I would have to put in later on. It was also, unfortunately, my parents' favourite time for Church, and for taking me also, so I had to tread warily here and not push my luck too far. I knew that attendance at Evening Service was more or less written in to my contract, so I never questioned that, but gradually I devised strategies to escape. My 'triumph' was to replace Sunday's evening service (6.30 to 7.45pm or much later if Mr Browne the Pastor got into his stride) with some other worthy event. So first I decided to visit other

Hall Street Baptist Church, setting for some merriment and numb bottoms, by Robbob

churches with a view to 'expanding my knowledge of the Christian faith'. (Just as boring as our Church.) and finally attending Epilogue at the YMCA (9 to 9.15 and coffee afterwards), a much shorter and more acceptable Christian occasion.

Saturday night was the 'big occasion' for getting spruced up, going out, and getting girls. Unfortunately while we were proficient in the first two activities, we were totally hopeless in the latter. At Church events or dances at the YM, we perfected a sort of 'staring routine'. This idiotic behaviour was intended to convey the 'girl-I-know-you-want-me-but-I'm–not-really-bothered' approach. The amount of time we spent in preparation, treating our teenage spots with 'Teencreem', and plastering our hair with 'Anzora' was out of all proportion to our success. 'Anzora' was a wonderful hair cream. In short, it set your hair very solidly in whatever style you chose. We must have looked like waxwork dummies with our smooth heads of hair. Gloves and a scarf were essential dress and, of course, B. Wilson had both yellow gloves and scarf. I had to settle for my dad's white silk dress scarf and any leather gloves I could scrounge, I think they were my mum's. Around that time, B. Wilson et al. started to go to dances at 'The Wigan Emp.' (Empire Ballroom). Such hedonistic jollification was not for me. (By order).

There were some sad moments in any weekend, which have always stuck in my memory. One was the acute feeling of angst when we were walking across King George VI playing fields late on Saturday, after a victorious match and the realisation that it would be a whole week before we would be playing again; second was the depressing sound of the opening chorus of 'Sing Something Simple' on the radio at 6 pm on Sunday evening, indicating that the doors of the schoolhouse (and later University) beckoned, and the solemn hymn at the end of Evening Service, 'The Day Thou Gavest Lord has ended' just about 'put the tin hat on it'.

Paul Feeney (2009) avers that the two most 'child-depressing' radio programmes ever made were 'Sing Something Simple' and the more awful 'Billy Cotton Band Show' and with this I heartily concur.

Wakey flippin' Wakey!

Onward to the GCE

ng Lit, Eng Lang, French, Geog, Hist, Latin, Maths, Physics; these were the eight subjects which I chose (joke) to study to GCE Ordinary Level. There was nothing ordinary about them for, as we were repeatedly told by staff, parents and other adults, it was on the results in these subjects that **our very lives and future happiness depended.** I was quite confident in the first six, at least they made some sort of sense, but Maths and Physics were going to be touch and go. Back in the 'real word', I was playing above my age in the St Helens 16–18 year league with the YM and pushing into the First XI in Cricket at school. At some stage I was also chosen to represent St Helens Schools in Athletics (high jump) but as the date clashed with a school cricket match I had, according to Fred (The Headmaster) 'remember my priorities' and so I backed out. (My interest in athletics was only rekindled as a Wycombe Phoenix Harrier in 1968, when I did beat Ken Friar's high jump mark).

Here I must mention two teachers who were outstanding, both in very different ways. George Tough (English) and Harry Siggers (French). Mr Tough, 'one of the Scottish Toughs', dark haired and moustachioed, 'sold' English Literature to us like no teacher I have ever had. One of the difficulties of the working class grammar school pupil was that, however well intentioned and enthusiastic our parents were, there was, generally, no home background in 'higher learning'. This lack of scholarship base was, and I think still is in evidence, at University interviews when one is asked about ones interests. (When asked at Leeds University what French authors I read 'for pleasure', I don't think my hesitant response carried much credence).

Mr Tough put this pleasure into English. We actually liked the poetry of John Milton, could recite *Comus, Lycidas, Il Penseroso et al* and understood all the literary allusions in them. Tough also had a wonderful line in banter. Eddie Duncan, the form comic, played 'Eric Morcambe' to Tough's 'Ernie Wise'. An exchange would be thus, 'Lycidas, he shall not remain unsung upon his watery bier' 'Greenalls Pale, Sir?' 'Not that sort of beer Duncan'. Tough also had some quotes for talkative boys, 'Mischance to him that gabbeth, would that he would hold his peace' and in the face of our unknowingness, 'O for a stone bow to hit him in t'th eye'. Or as Eddie would put it, after some disturbance, 'I think its time for that stone bow, Sir.'

He was also possessed of uncanny prescience. On one occasion, when he was our form teacher, we were waiting for him to take afternoon registration. Waiting comprised the usual hurling of objects around the classroom while we sheltered behind our desk lids. On this particular afternoon someone had introduced a rugby ball into the array of missiles, and one well-aimed throw hit Eddie Duncan on the head and to our amazement/joy/ consternation richocheted up and demolished the globe lampshade on the ceiling. All hands to the pumps, we cleared all the glass away and, with all evidence removed sat meekly to await Tough's arrival. He walked straight though the door, looked up at the naked bulb, and said, 'Duncan was that you?'

Harry Siggers was of a different kidney. Like Tough he knew and loved his subject but his method of involving us was to insult us. He looked on us as 'oiks' who needed to be liberated from the cultural wasteland of St Helens. 'The other day I went into a grocer's shop in St Helens and asked the girl what cheeses they sold. She said, 'We just sell cheese'. How can you live in a place like this?' (Roars of laughter.) 'French, promise me that before I die you will leave this benighted town'. He had some good throwaway lines. He would be in the middle of some explanation or other and would say, 'this author's work has been compared to Shakespeare. You do remember Shakespeare, don't you, Rawlinson, famous twelfth century Persian conqueror'. He was into all forms of 'culture'. 'On Saturday I am going to the Walker Art Gallery in Liverpool. If any of you morons would like to accompany me, I will attempt to explain Modern Art.' So we toddled along behind his homburged and gloved figure and he gave us a complete grounding in the subject.

He was also magnificently rude. What teacher today would be able to pronounce, 'You know boys there is nothing in this world as good as having a bash with your wife?' Looking back over the terms leading up to the GCE, I am quite surprised that I cannot remember much in the vivid way I have described the earlier years. Perhaps there was less trauma. My weeks were very, very predictable. (In fact I recently learned that I lived through The Most Boring Day in History which has been calculated by W Tunstall-Pedoe as April 12 1954. Nothing happened of any consequence in the whole world. As that was a Sunday I'm not surprised. Nothing ever happened on any Sunday in St Helens.)

School days continued in time to the inexorable 'Time Table'. In the evenings, Monday to Thursday was homework; Friday was Youth Club at Church (badminton and mild flirting) Saturday was YMCA, soccer or cricket and Sunday was – more homework. I should have got the Nobel Homework Prize, had there been one. Yet my life was just the same as all my Cowley compatriots, as it was for those studying at Cowley Girls Grammar, West Park Boys Catholic Grammar, and The Convent (Catholic Girls Grammar). We were put on this earth to study and pass exams. An anonymous poem in the *Cowley Girls School Magazine* sums up our plight to perfection:-

Lack of Leisure
What is this life if we've no play,
Just work and more work every day?
No time for pictures, books or pop,
Just Latin, French, Maths till we drop.
No time to dance or make a date,
With all our work we'd turn up late.
No time with friends to have a chat,
Or even wield a rounders bat.
No time to sit or sew or view
Each wasted second we would rue.
No time to run or jump or leap,

Just English, Science, till we sleep
A poor life this if we've no play
Just work and more work every day

Anon

In response to my protestations about 'social development' we were told we could 'develop' later. When you've got your Degree'. Here was the more or less 'hidden' problem in a selective Grammar School. No one paid the slightest interest to you as a developing person, you were a developing scholar or developing sportsman, preferably both. The concept of 'personal and social development' which was to sweep into education in the latter part of the century, a concept which many Grammar school alumni fervently espoused as future educators (almost as 'revenge' for our treatment), was unknown. My cousin Marie, the same age as myself, a pupil at the Central Modern School, studied something called 'Social Studies'. They actually looked at events which were current and affecting the society we lived in. To me this seemed eminently interesting but in response to my questions I was told that it was 'hardly academic'.

A clash of cultures ▌ ▌ ▌ ▌ ▌

One memorable event occurred in the early summer of 1956. It was a small thing in itself but it was illustrative of the gulf between, shall we say 'Town and Gown', between what the School saw as its purpose for us, and what we saw as our purpose, or perhaps complete lack of. On Saturday April 28 1956, in the early days of the cricket season, Cowley had a First XI fixture against the neighbouring Prescot Grammar School. In a parallel world, April 28 1956 was to be the 'Day of Reckoning', 'Saints' v Halifax at Wembley Stadium, the Final of the Rugby League Challenge Trophy. Everybody and his granddad had got tickets for the match, at which St Helens was going to avenge the ignominious defeat of 1953 by Huddersfield.

In our innocence we thought nothing of it. The match (our insignificant cricket match) could be rearranged and obviously would be, in the light of this momentous event. As Captain I was delegated to have a word with Pam (Mr Morley) and sort it out. I explained our predicament and waited for the expected answer. Only it was not the answer I expected. He slowly began to get angry... 'The status of cricket in this school'.... and angrier... 'all this school has given you'.... and blazing ... 'and you of all people, a Colours man' etc etc (*So that's a no then?*). I returned and told my dejected XI that we would have to play the match. With the threat of strike action in the air, a few uncomfortable days passed. I was then summoned to Pam's presence and informed that he had had a phone call from Prescot Grammar to say that they could not fulfil the fixture because ... (wait for it.). '**they were all going to the Rugby League Cup Final**'.

Straight faces had to be kept, but that was a victory for common sense.

The day out at Wembley was memorable. I well remember climbing up a long series of covered steps to reach our spectating

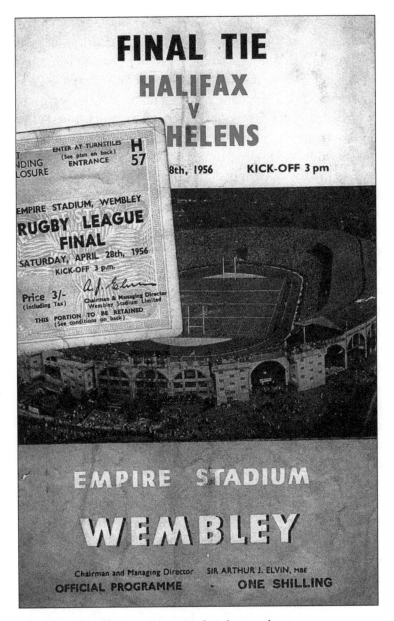

The Wembley Programme and ticket stub

spot and coming out at the very top of the stadium. Looking down on this huge bowl, the green field with its white markings, did take one's breath away. I had never seen anything as huge. Although Saints won the match by 13 points to 2, for well over half the game Halifax led by a solitary penalty goal. Our hapless (*'ees bloody 'opeless*) scrum half Austin Rhodes missed several quite easy penalties causing one gent standing in front of us to throw his rosette onto the floor and grind it underfoot. Were we going to 'bottle' another Wembley appearance? Then, with about half an hour left to play, transformation. Frank Carlton on the left wing finally outstripped the tiring Halfax defence and crossed for a try. And, from a difficult position, the previously clueless Rhodes added the conversion. When Steve Llewellyn, scored one of his signature diving tries we knew it was all over. Rhodes, (*'ees magnificent*), kicked all the conversions, and the now exuberant gent in front of us calmly took a rosette out of some stranger's lapel and put it in his own. A day to remember. (Most definitely better than cricket.)

A cricketing event to remember for all the wrong reasons, was our day out at Old Trafford, the Lancashire County Ground, to watch Lancashire versus the Australian tourists. So myself, Eddie Duncan, Brian Wilson and Micky Daybell, took the train to Manchester and, for some reason, walked from the Victoria Station to Old Trafford. The nearer we got to the ground, the darker the skies became and as we paid our entrance money the drizzle began. We sat in our macs, happily munching our sandwiches and waited for the rain to stop and play to begin. The rain stopped, the umpires came out, went back in and an announcement followed that a further inspection would be held at 12.00 noon. The rain started again and by 3 pm we decided to call it quits. The journey home was more eventful than the non-cricket, as we met some junior Cowley 'tick' on the train, who was actually wearing his school cap. Cue silliness; cap taken from head of boy and passed round the compartment; cap then jammed in train window just needing one touch to send it flying into the blue; someone (OK I confess) applied the touch and said cap vanished. 'His mother will kill you.'

The coda to this washout was that the game was also due to be televised and, as you might guess, three very damp boys arrived home just in time to see on TV, at 4.30 pm, the first balls of the day bowled on a sawdust covered Old Trafford pitch.

(Dad thought it was hilarious)

Piece of cake really ▪ ▪ ▪ ▪ ▪

To my amazement I passed all the eight 'O' level subjects, even Physics and the dreaded Maths. I remember the sinking feeling going through the Maths paper with maths supremo Brian Wilson in the bike sheds after the exam. (Why was he good at the things I wasn't?) My answers didn't seem to be anything like his. This meant that until the results came out I could dwell on the prospect of failure at any time I chose to torment myself. I vowed then that I would never succumb to the temptation of this type of hysterical analysis again and it has always served me in good stead. The valiant taste of death but once. After the euphoria of the result however, I suddenly felt quite 'down'. Five years of slog and what now – another two of even harder 'A' Level slog, cheered by the encouragement of our mentors, 'You will never, in your life, work as hard as you will in these next two years.' Oh gee thanks. (Actually it was true.)

Rebellion was now in the air. My first attempt to challenge authority was to announce that I did not want to go to Torquay on our family holiday but to go to Butlins like all other sane individuals. This was vetoed by The Lord Protector Cromwell (my dad), so I added the dire threat that as I had no choice but to attend this sham holiday, I did not want to be seen in their company. Trying to avoid ones parents is difficult at the best of times, but finding them sitting behind you in a Paignton cinema during a showing of *Gunfight at the OK Corral* was the limit. A truce was called. (In the event, Dad's minor triumph was to discover that one of the Butlins holidaymakers went to sleep for a week after returning from his holiday.)

On returning home, I then announced that I was going to leave school and 'get a job' as I was 'fed up' with school. A mate down the road had passed all his exams, **and** left, **and** got a job at Pilkingtons Glassworks. (This was not hard to do as everybody in St Helens worked at Pilks). Now while dad didn't mind what I did 'as long as I was happy', he always deferred to mum in real decisions. ('Your mum knows a thing or two'). Mum was always the politician. She just asked me what job I was thinking of doing, and as I hadn't got the foggiest idea, suggested that I should go back into the sixth form so that I could keep my options open until I made my mind up. There was no logical way I could counter this proposal, so back I went. As the 'wise woman' had worked out, the 'job' would soon be forgotten.

The Sixth Form

I t was at this time that factors combined to transform my Cowley experience from 'Dotheboys Hall' to the 'Elyssian Fields'. Over the vacation the staff, like Bottom the Weaver, had become 'translated'. They all were friendly, called you by your Christian name, and generally assumed a 'one of us' attitude. A cynic might say that as Sixth Formers we were worth a lot of financial points to the school, *ergo* it was in the school's interest that we were cosseted. However the attitude was much more relaxed.

At the same time I started to hit my growth spurt (about bloody time too). I put on weight and inches to my height reaching the 5' 10" mark and found myself taller than some of those who had been 'gigantic' in the lower school. (So, no more sand in the face). I had also become much more active in the YMCA, taking football coaching sessions, assisting at the annual camps at Lakeside and Newcastle (N. Ireland), leading folk singing sessions on the guitar. So things were looking up all round.

(In fact the YMCA was my 'road not taken'. Bill Leyland definitely wanted me to enter the Association with a view to becoming a General Secretary. The problems were that I knew that the Gen. Sec. wages at the time were a pittance even compared to a teacher's, hopefully my first choice of career, and, the further blocker for me was that to join the Association as a 'Full Member' you had to make some statement about belief in God (The 'C' in the YMCA) and I just could not do it. So despite being active in the YM all the way through School, University and as long as I lived in St Helens, I never went 'the whole hog' – but then again I've never been a whole hogger.)

Back to the Sixth Form; The first bit of local difficulty was choosing which of 'A' level subjects on offer we were going to study. It was general practice that we would study three subjects

106

at 'A' level as it was thought that the work load would be appropriate. But, after waving a gleeful goodbye to Maths and Physics, what should I pick out of the remaining five (Eng Lang and Lit being combined)? Now it was the policy of the school **not** to tell you your marks in the exam. The main aim was, quite sensibly, that you should study subjects that you liked and not subjects that, on the strength of one examination, you had got 'good marks' in. On the subjects-u-like criteria, I would then pick English, French plus History. But what about Latin? My Latin mark, which I wheedled out of 'Kipper' was above distinction level, far and away better than any of my other subjects, and as my mate, Brian Wilson, said if you do French and English you would be swamped with set books. (This coming from someone who did 'A' level Art, the cushiest number known to man). So Latin **had** to be in. In the end I opted for Latin, French and History. This brought a rollicking from Mr Tough (English) who said I was a 'bloody idiot'.

Of course the underlying problem was making a choice between 'a' or 'b' when unfortunately you can't have both, and, something I learned much, much later, that there is a consequence of choosing, i.e. 'opportunity costs'. By choosing 'a' you have to give up what you could have had if you had chosen 'b', **and accept it.** (In a memorable management training film of the 1980's John Cleese, as St Peter, explains this to a harassed manager (James Bolam) who has had a (divinely induced) heart attack, brought on by not being able to make decisions. 'You have to make choices. **Its called Growing Up!'**) This statement of the 'bleeding obvious' would have been so helpful for me then.

'*Alfred Arthur Lynch, you have been tried fairly before this court and it is now my duty to pass sentence upon you*'. This, would you believe, was the start of a piece of prose which not only did we have to translate into Latin but we also had to transpose into the Roman vernacular. (They said 'A' Level was hard.) So before we could get down to the language we had to decide on which one of the many Romans this sentence could be passed and make sure that all the language we used could have been used by a Roman court. I think I went for 'Coriolanus'.

This was something we did every fortnight for two years, interposed with translating 'set books', Ovid *Metamorphosis*, Virgil *Aeneas* and *Georgics IV*, Tacitus *Agricola*, and conning up all the allusions therein and being able to recite Latin poetry in the appropriate Latin metre. 'Dactyls', 'spondees' you name 'em we did 'em. It was during this sixth form experience that we were to witness the High Noon (Altus Noonus), the denoument of a long running feud between the venerable 'Kipper' Addshead and the unfathomable Reg Holme. In a nutshell they did not get on. Now I don't know if Reg did pass Latin, but I do remember 'Kipper' getting his rag out about the possibility of one of his charges (Reg) actually having the intention to fail. I, unwittingly, got caught (literally as they say) in the middle of this during one session in which 'Kipper' was talking about the Roman legion. Somehow he moved to his experiences in The War 1914-18. It could have been the Hundred Years War for all we knew. He said that if the battalion was having rabbit stew for dinner then whoever was serving the meal got the rabbits head. I was sitting in the front desk, about a foot from 'Kipper', and Reg was sitting right behind me. 'Aye', whispered Reg in my ear, 'an' its fucking well growed on you.' The symbolism between the cadaverous 'Kipper and a rabbit's head was perfect. But I was in no position to celebrate Reg's explosive dart. I just had to keep a straight face while every part of my body was shaking with mirth.

French with Harry rolled along. We were fortunate to have Maupassant's *Quinze Contes* as a 'set book', and *Vol de Nuit* by St Exupery. These were superb stories in themselves – and dead easy to translate. *La Parure, Boule de Suif* and *La Vedette* are still easy to recall, and *Sur l'eau*, the story of the terrifying night on the river with its denoument of a body dragged up on the anchor in the morning sunshine, still makes your hairs stand up. The other set books were a bit 'mancky'. *Le Crime de Sylvestre Bonnard* (Anatole France) boring, *Le Medecin Malgre Lui* (Moliere) sooo not funny *and Atala et Rene dans Les Natchez* (Rousseau) (Why?). Somebody should tell the French that their literature is crap.

The Sixth Form (V1 A Modern) with Kipper.

back row Birchall, Heath, Birkett, Shaw, Fielding, Rawlinson,
    Holmes, Wilson, Parr
front row Fackey, ??, Kilshaw, Clarke, Mr Addshead, French RJ,
    Dixon, Middlehurst, French B

We went to see the Moliere's *Tartuffe* at the Liverpool
Everyman Theatre. The event was marked by the disappearance
of Keith (Almond First XI cricket Captain and jazz clarinetist) and
the upper sixth contingent into the depths of Yates' Wine Lodge.
But we did go on the train, which allowed some of our foremost
scholars to divert themselves by throwing the light bulbs out
of the window on the return journey. (The comedian Alexi
Sayle recalls a similar incident, at the Liverpool Everyman, when
one of his well soused fellow students told the Prologue to Henry
V, (O! for a muse of fire), to 'Fuck Off' and spent the afternoon
being chased round the theatre by ushers.)

In the vanguard of educational reform, it was decide that to
broaden our narrowing outlook on scholarship, we should all
undertake something called 'General Studies' at 'O' Level.
Ostensibly this was to encourage (make) VI Form 'Arts' students
do a bit of science, and 'Science' students to study the arts. There
were a series of lectures each week. I recall one session in which
someone came in and made a fibreglass canoe, explaining the
chemical processes that were involved in mixing and producing

this rock solid medium. We could have been the first sixth form zonked out by the toxic fumes. We also had to produce a project (very novel) on some scientific topic. Mine was 'The International Geophysical Year'; sounds great; can't remember anything else; must have been memorable. What I did remember was a 'Field Trip' to Ingleborough's cave complex and Gaping Gill in far off Yorkshire. It was a fair trek – no motorways then – so plenty of time to establish the usual card school at the back of the coach. Doing his educational duty at the front, one of the geography staff pointed out the various places of interest viz; glacial valleys and ox bow lakes. At some point he stopped his discursion and asked whether anyone had anything to add. Now I swear that this was not in anyway calculated, but breaking the silence that followed his question, a sonorous voice from the card school in the rear said, 'pay twenty ones'.

The return journey was no less diverting. As many of the party, especially the card school had imbibed a fair amount of liquid at lunch and beyond, the need to 'stop the bus' became paramount. Now 'Paddy' Moss told us that we should 'go' before we set off. This we all duly did, but some bladders were weaker or fuller than others. Graham Leadbetter grew increasingly agitated as the journey wore on and was worried that his kidneys were going to pack in if help was not forthcoming. Chants down the coach to the tune of, 'Are we stopping, Mr Moss', were received with a smile and a wave from 'Paddy'. As we used to write in our science books, 'A bottle was obtained', and a relieved 'Leddy' was able to fill it. 'Put the top back on and empty it when we get back', was our advice. All was well: but the journey home is always longer than the journey out and 'Leddy's' cup to began to o'erfill. No other bottle could be found for his second evacuation, and so, showing the instantaneous decision making skills that epitomised the Cowleian, he slipped back the window and emptied the contents into the wind, which to our amusement and horror splattered the windscreen of a following vehicle. On behalf of the lower sixth, I apologise to you sir, whoever you were.

At about this time it was suggested by our 'careers advisor' (forgive me while I titter) that we should start thinking about

University applications. Now the post of Careers Advisor in Grammar School was the same as Citizenship Tutor in today's educational mess; a) a joke; b) unstructured; c) unwanted; d) given to a new teacher. At that time I was keen to take French. I liked the language, I like all foreign languages, but the 'best' Universities already had their own exams in place for each subject especially at 'Honours level', and so I applied for London. I was duly sent a test paper to sit at school, which was a translation from and into French. It was a stinker, more 'S' level that 'A'. I really struggled with it and I knew from the off that I was not going to 'the Smoke'.

My next application was Leeds Uni. Here fortune smiled sweetly, but by default. Mike Heath, a class mate and cricketing colleague, had already applied for Leeds and taken their test. 'So what sort of things did they ask, Mike?' 'Oh', said Mike, 'I've kept the paper, here, have a look'. So I did. The standard was not as high as London but there were some rather arcane bits in it like 'le bossu', 'the dwarf'. So come the day of the Leeds exam; well, bugger me, they've sent the exact paper they gave Mike Heath. **Huge Moral Dilemma;** should I sit this paper or declare it invalid because of my prior knowledge? That internal debate lasted about two seconds. This was a gift horse and should be well ridden. So I romped through the paper, making sure to make just a few minor errors (If I put 'dwarf' for 'le bossu' will it give the game away? I think I went for something like 'small man') Any way I got an interview at Leeds – and yet the sods still wanted 65% in French and 60% in History and Latin.

'Are you in love French?' 'No Sir' 'Well I think you are going orff'. This was Harry Siggers' analysis of my state of health as we entered the home stretch of the 'A' Levels in 1958. I had no idea I was going orff. I just didn't feel confident about my future performance in the 'A' level exams. I haven't a clue why? Maybe the idea of 'University' was a little daunting. I was applying to these unfamiliar places Leicester, Leeds, Durham. 'Why not Liverpool or Manchester?' said mum. 'Wouldn't have a chance'. Maybe I **was** just bombed out with study. Looking back I don't know why I was not confident. I had just got into a groove, which said, 'You're not good enough.' I suppose, because of the perfectionist streak, I felt that, as I had no real 'love' for academia, or the 'academia' I was offered, I was really morally cheating. Indeed in my interview at Leeds, I was thrown by the question, 'Are you telling me you read Maupassant for pleasure?' I felt that the interviewers actually did read French for pleasure, but that I read it to get into University, pleasurable or not. Maybe I was running up against the 'class system', which we thought the 'eleven plus exam' had abolished. 'Top' universities were decidedly upper/middle class and strove to maintain their position. (In fact even as late as 1962 I was told in interview by the principal of a mere 'College', that I would just have to lose my 'Lancashire accent'. I didn't have a Lancashire accent anyway, it was a well honed nasal St Helenian – Scouse. Had I had a proper Lancashire accent I could have made a fortune demolishing chimneys and driving round Bolton on my steam roller.)

Any road up, on we bashed and 'A' levels came and were passed. As I could have predicted, an easy 'Distinction' in Latin, but only 55% in French and a crazy 45% in History. So bang went the Leeds place; now what? At that time applications were made to a specific Universities Honours school. There was then no Clearing House System nor any means by which one university could pass your form on to another. So one was faced with a mad round of desperate form filling. Leicester nothing, Nottingham same, what about Scotland, four year courses, but you got a Masters Degree.

To get into a Scottish University you had to go through another round of Scot's bureaucracy and first apply to the Scottish Universities Exam Board for something called *The Attestation of Fitness Certificate for Entry to a Scottish University*. This was the longest brag sheet I have ever penned, listing all my 'O' Level and 'A' level passes, and it had bugger all influence. Dundee nothing, Aberdeen nothing, St Andrews nothing. ('Will ye no come back again?' No I sodding well wont.) Harry Siggers valiantly tried to lift my mood by suggesting that as I was only 5% off the Leeds mark in French and had got a creditable 45% in French at 'S' Level, he would ask his mate at London, who was an

Admissions Tutor for French, to see what could be done. In the face of this eminently practical suggestion I reacted like the serious minded pillock I was, and said that this would smack of favouritism. In my mind I was finished with French for good and Latin was the 'obvious' subject to study. 'Kipper' said that with the marks I had already had I would walk into any Latin Department, probably without an interview. Now that's what I wanted to hear.

Out of a clear
blue sky...

On I Feb 1958, Manchester United's *Busby Babes* defeated Arsenal 5–4 on a mud heap of a pitch before a crowd of over 60,000. Following this triumph, United flew out to Belgrade where the 3–3 draw with Red Star saw them through to the semi finals of the European Cup.

On a cold Thursday afternoon (the sixth) I was returning home on one of the two bus routes that passed near our house. Waiting on the step for the bus to stop, the conductor looked at me and said, 'What a tragedy.' I was a bit taken a back by this statement and just responded, 'What tragedy?' 'Man U., big plane crash, some dead, lots injured'. It was an unbelievable story. The crash had happened due to snow and icing on the runway at Munich, and the plane had failed to get lift off. Amid all the rumours, we gathered that seven of the team were dead but Bobby Charlton was unhurt and Matt Busby and Duncan Edwards were alive but in hospital. Eleven journalists died including Frank Swift, the ex Man City goalkeeper. The dead were flown back to Manchester on the eleventh and thousands stood in the freezing rain to pay their respects. Later we learned that Matt Busby was alive, but that Duncan Edwards, a symbol of the new footballing youth had died. This event paralysed the North of England. Newspapers were full of the story and daily bulletins were issued, especially keeping track of Matt Busby's progress.

But of course life must go on, and so the next question for footballing minds was, "Can Man U. still win the FA Cup?" Of course the whole of the footballing population were willing that this could be so. When a makeshift United side beat Sheffield Wednesday in the semi-final 3–0, then winning the Cup was a near certainty. The Bolton team were all affected by this situation. Many players confessed to weeping on the team coach as it journeyed up Wembley Way. However, professionalism reasserted itself, and Bolton ended all our dreams with two goals scored by Nat Lofthouse, although even he was concerned about doing the traditional lap of honour with the Cup.

The best days of my life (and a girl friend at last.)

A
nd so it came to pass that I returned to Cowley in the autumn of 1958 to reapply to University and to retake my 'A' levels 'to improve my grades'. I was now a prefect and Deputy Head Boy – there was no one else left, only the brilliant Bill Tunstall who was Head Boy. I was summoned to the Head's study for a chat. Somewhere along the route we had acquired a new head called Wright. He was a very, very rotund Yorkshire man with jowls. We called him 'Fred' after Fred Emney, the monacled, cigar-smoking comedian. He also was interested in Cricket, on which all Yorkshire men tiresomely pontificate, and was insistent that my long run up should be curtailed by half. Now maybe I was a bit 'fattist' but I could not quite see 'Fred' as a sporting role model. I never really hit it off with him, the pattern being set when he interrupted a flourishing card school in the Senior Library and as all the participants stood up in respect, money trickled out of their quickly slammed exercise books and bounced along the desks. I was decidedly a non-gambler (too mean) and was sitting over by a bookcase. He just looked at me and said, 'Why is it French, that every time I come in here you are lurking round a corner?' 'Coincidence, Sir', I replied my steely blue gaze unflinching. The import of his 'chat' was that I should be working even harder to improve my grades and not slacking and, 'Promise me this, French, when you get to University you will not take your guitar'. (Weird).

On the sporting front, soccer became even more thrilling, if that were possible. One of my footballing mates was a boy called Geoff Finney. Although probably not related to the immortal Tom Finney of Preston North End, his cousin Ken currently played as a professional for Stockport County. Geoff was a very talented player (I hate to say but a far better player than I was).

The Prefects with Fred 1959
back row Davies, Dixon, French RJ, French B, ??
front row Sharrock, Fielding, Clarke, The Head, Tunstall, Parr,
　　　　　Middlehurst

Out of the blue, Geoff's uncle suggested that Geoff and I should
go up to Wigan Athletic, as he could arrange a trial for us. I was
over the moon at this and amazed when Geoff said he wasn't
interested. Wigan Athletic, with a proper ground at Springfield
Park was a coming force in the Lancashire Combination and
had just been taken over by Malcolm Barass, the ex Bolton
Wanderers centre-half. So off I toddled with my bag and after lots
of practice games, (unfortunately not on the main pitch), I was
called up to the manager's office in the Main Stand. 'We'd like you
to sign Lancs Combi forms for us, Brian,' said Malcolm. And to
the singing of all the choirs in heaven I duly did. I played against
the first team in the 'public practice' match and was selected to
play in the Reserves against – St Helens Town.
　　　So on one hot late summer afternoon I walked onto the 'Field
of Dreams' lining up at right-wing, ready to do my bit. Soon in the
first-half I got my chance. I pushed the ball past their labouring
full-back, cut inside their centre-half and angled in on goal.
Then, to the groans of the assembled, rather than smash the ball
into the net, I passed the ball across the face of the goal. In football terms it's called 'Passing the Responsibility'. I was the player

'who-can-do-anything-in-training-but-can't-deliver-on-the-pitch', an unfortunate character trait, which I had to work hard on in my adult football career. But there it was. I had two more games against Morris Motors and Stalybridge and then faded into oblivion. Put simply, the more important something, was the more I was likely to 'freeze'. This I think is the difference between us mortals and top sports men. They are nerveless, (and probably thick.)

Back at school there was another diversion, which had most unforeseen but pleasant consequences. Granada TV used to run a series of talk shows called *Youth Wants An Answer*, and we were informed that one of the shows was to feature a team from the combined forces of Cowley Boys and Girls Schools, two pupils from each school. After a round of classroom discussions with the producers, I was selected as one of the team. We were all agog to know what out 'challenging topic' was to be and which 'celebrity' was to field our penetrating questions. We were informed that our 'hot topic' was to be The Hospital System (deep joy) and the celebrity was Mr Unknown. Despite this initial anticlimax, we enjoyed ourselves at Granada studios in Manchester and the show passed without a hitch, apart from Ricky Rawlinson's comment to me that his dad said I 'sounded like a bloody miner'. Jealousy, boys, jealousy. I was also almost petrified with stage fright, (the big occasion syndrome). The other object of interest for me was one of my teammates from the Girls School. She was a tall dark haired girl, very amiable, and as far as my gauchness allowed, we got on well, and her name was Marie (pronounced Mari) and .... nothing happened.

Bill 'Genius' Tunstall passed the Cambridge Entrance Exam and thus avoided the 'A' Level exams, meaning he would leave school at Christmas 1958, which would leave me as Head Boy by default. Before he left he had to organise the Prefect's Dance, (now I believe it's called The Prom and costs parents a fortune). It was THE event of the year and he took it upon himself to find me a partner. Let me say that in the mating game, Bill was the only boy I knew apart from Mike Heath, who actually had such a priceless thing as a girlfriend and I am quite certain that his relationship was more than platonic. 'Look', he said, 'you're Deputy Head Boy, you're organizing this, you have to go and you have to have a partner. I'll ask my sister to sort something out.' Soon of course, came the suggestion that I should go with 'that girl you were on TV with. You'll be OK there.' And so it was. I partnered Mari to the 'Pre's Dance' and 'the best days of my life' began. To actually have a girlfriend was a price beyond rubies, especially that sublime moment when you hold her hand, you squeeze her hand and .... she squeezes yours. We were fairly inseparable from then on, after I had summoned up enough courage to tell my dad. Long walks in dark parks; back (double) seats of the *Rivoli* Cinema where we didn't even remember what was on; romantic journeys to Blackpool versus Everton; St Helens versus Halifax at Osdal Stadium, Bradford, with a meal afterwards at the 'Flying Horse'; popping down to Mari's at 8.45 in the evening which involved two cross town buses, a quick good night' snog and two buses back; listening to 'Scherezade' while her dad and mum were at the pub. Mari, who went on to become one of the leading head teachers in St Helens, had something that may only be found in Lancastrians, self deprecating humour, a very precious and wining quality.

In January of 1959, a small envelope dropped through the letterbox. On a typed copy were the words;-

'Kings College, in the University of Durham, are pleased to offer you an unconditional place in the Department of Classics'. We would be pleased if you would confirm your acceptance of this offer'

Yippee! Let joy be unconfined. I was IN at long bloody last. So with my place at Newcastle confirmed, I rather thought that in the manner of Bill Tunstall, I would leave school as there was no point in improving my grades as it did not now matter. 'Fred' would have none of it. For some reason he came up with this strange argument that St Helens Education Authority would only fund a scholarship concurrent with the year of the examination. He argued that I may not get the Award for 1959 if I left school with my 1958 'A' levels. This was really the most sublime tosh I had ever heard. To this day I don't know what his real reason was. Maybe he thought I would become a guitar addicted hippie drop-out if not constantly monitored or, more likely he would lose 'points' (and money) in the Schools rating system.

So I continued as before and, for what it was worth, passed the damn A levels again, probably becoming the only person in Great Britain who has 'A' Levels squared. In their wisdom the examiners altered the instructions in the 'Latin 1' paper. We were asked to answer only **Two** questions instead of the usual **Three**. 'I suppose you answered all three questions, French?' sighed 'Kipper'. I had of course just beavered away regardless. 'Read the rubric.' he admonished, and to this day I have. I did much better in French and History but marginally worse in Latin. No matter, I carried on, incurring Sarky's sneer when I turned up late for assembly on my first day as Head Boy. 'I though you were Head Boy, French, I must have got it wrong.' I continued to 'terrify' local batsmen with my long run up, a fact I learned much later from the lawyer who was looking after my mother's will, who happened to have been the captain of Prescot Grammar First XI. In athletics, I swept the board at the School Sports winning 100, 200, hurdles, high jump and long jump, before proud Mum and Dad and the wonderful Mari. Could life get any better?

Bibliography

Buckton H. (2009) *The Children's Front* (The impact of WWII on British children) Philimore and Co, Chichester.

Feeney P. (2009) *A 1950s Childhood.* History Press.

Hall D. (2014) *Working Lives,* Corgi Books

Hanson Michelle (2012*) What the Grown-Ups Were Doing,* (An Odyssey through 1950s Suburbia.) Simon and Schuster.

Hennessy P. (2006) *Having it so good.* Allen Lane/Penguin.

Kynaston D. (2007) *Smoke in The Valley* (Austerity Britain 1948–51) Bloomsbury.

" " (2009) *Family Britain 1951-1957* Bloomsbury

" " (2013) *Modernity Britain* (Opening the Box 1957-59 Bloomsbury

Menzies Barbara (1997) *I thought as a child.* Countrywise Ltd

O'Neil B. (2014) *I'm a godless survivor of Faith Schools.* Big Issue June 16-22

Tucker A. (2014) *Head Cook and Bottle Washer.* (Growing up in post war St Helens) P3 Publications. Carlisle.

Turner B. (2011) *Beacon for change; How the festival of Britain shaped the modern age.* Aurum Press Ltd.

Wilson A. N. (2008) *Our Times; the Age of Elizabeth II.* Hutchinson

The School Song

In our work and in our leisure
May we help the School's good name
Seeking not a selfish pleasure
Seeking not a selfish fame
But by doing all things well
Fearing not the truth to tell
We will help the School to swell
The name of Cowley

Other boys have gone before us
And left their mark behind
But their spirit still is o'er us
And we keep them still in mind
Carry on their work aright
One and all with main and might
Strive to keep the 'scutcheon bright
The fame of Cowley

To the boys who follow later
We will leave a record clean
A tradition growing greater
And a spirit true and keen
Thus united with the past
And the future firm and fast
We'll uphold until the last
The name of Cowley

Lightning Source UK Ltd.
Milton Keynes UK
UKHW020316190321
380584UK00001B/9